CONTENTS

INTRODUCTION

I've had two beginnings when it comes to bowhunting public land whitetails. As a 12-year old first-timer, I occasionally hunted public land around Lanesboro, Minnesota, with my father. The land, which was near a few patches of private on which we could bowhunt, was good enough for us then to spend some treestand time.

Try as I might, I can only recall one deer that we ever killed on public land, and that was a button buck my father arrowed one evening. I never shot a deer on public land during those early years, but to be honest, I never shot one on private either. Not until I was four seasons into it, at least.

And that, too, was a button buck.

I do remember plenty of good hunts on public land, just as I remember plenty that went the other way. It's not hard to conjure memories of the young bucks I missed on a particular stretch of public land that bordered the Root River and was always good for a sighting or two.

I can easily recall a two-year-old buck that frequented a spot that is now off-limits to hunting. My father and I hunted that deer with as many plans as we could come up with, and while he wasn't the safest 100-inch eight-pointer out there, he wasn't in much danger from the Peterson crew.

At that time, at least during the first two full seasons, we also had an awful lot of private land to roam as well. Then, when I was fourteen years old and looking forward to another whitetail season, one of the farms ended up selling. The new owners were nice, but they were also bowhunters, and you can guess how that went for us.

We still had plenty of other ground, all located around a cabin that my father's friend owned. Until, that is, he too decided he was going to close up shop, at least as far as we were concerned. We went from having nearly too much private land to bowhunt to having none in the span of a couple of weeks.

That meant we were relegated to public only, and I'll never forget sitting in the pounding rain on opening morning and watching ghostly faces creep closer to my stand through the downpour. The squirrel hunters had camouflage raingear (no blaze orange), and only their faces seem to show through the rain. It was one of those times where they were on me before I could signal that I was 14 feet over their heads, and by then, I just sat still and let them pass out of fear of drawing attention to myself and resembling, just a little too much, a bushytail.

If you bowhunt deer enough, you'll know frustration in its purest form. It took me three seasons to get there. We didn't stop hunting, but the reality of killing any deer with a sharp stick seemed far-fetched. Even then, bowhunting was something that was in my blood in a way that nothing else has ever been. It's gene-deep and not something you'll catch me apologizing for—ever.

It goes without saying that during school I talked about bowhunting. A lot. And it was one of those times, during study hall if I remember correctly, that a fellow classmate casually asked me if I was bowhunting his family farm.

He'd given us permission to turkey hunt there that spring, and the spring before, but we hadn't asked them if we could deer hunt, so his offer came as a surprise. I told him in no uncertain terms that we'd love to bowhunt his farm. He said he'd let his dad know.

Just like that, we went from having no private ground to a farm that I could scarcely believe. And so our public stint ended with a fizzle because we had very little reason to go where others could when we had freedom to tread where others couldn't.

Throughout two decades of bowhunting, I focused on that farm and a few others that I gained permission to hunt. In 2006 I ended up getting my dream job as Associate Editor for *Petersen's Bowhunting Magazine* and, quite frankly, figured any reason I had of ever having to slum it again on public ground was gone.

Through that job, I learned a lot about the hunting industry and a lot about the most famous bowhunters out there. While plenty of it was positive, I realized that most of the folks tasked with giving hunting advice were also hunting the best land—and the dumbest deer—possible.

It started to bother me that most of the whitetail experts in the industry were hunting the least challenging deer out there. After all, where else can you become an expert by taking the easiest possible way to get there?

For two years I worked that job until the housing market collapsed, the stock market dropped quicker than a spine-shot buck, and the print industry realized how shaky its foundation really was. Out the door I went, along with about 40 percent of the people in our company. Having had a taste of the good life, I wanted to stay in the industry, and the only way to do it was to become a freelance writer and photographer.

That's what I did, until I realized that I was going to starve without more assignments. I needed more work. More recognition.

Enter my second beginning on public land.

I realized that there was an opportunity for someone in the hunting industry to make a name for himself hunting public land deer. At that time my wife and I didn't have any kids, and I didn't have a whole lot to lose by focusing a year on killing a mature buck or two where other writers and industry members wouldn't hunt.

If I'm being totally honest, I did it only partially for business. A big driver in my decision was ego. I had some people tell me that what I wanted to do couldn't be done, and I wanted to show them they were wrong. I wanted to be able to throw a pair of middle fingers up in the air and aim them squarely at the hunting industry. And, honestly, I wanted to focus on killing good bucks on common dirt just to see if I could.

To prove it to myself.

I'm not lying when I say that it took me four days of scouting and a full day of hunting that first year to kill a 138-inch deer. That North Dakota eight-pointer, who couldn't help but cross the same spot on the Little Missouri River each night and morning, solidified something in me that I've always suspected but had never fully understood.

Good whitetail hunts can be had on public land. A bowhunter willing to put in the time can have a quality experience whitetail hunting Uncle Sam's ground. Of course, that first hunt was a gift. It's rarely that easy, although I'm finding that quick success isn't quite as uncommon as one would assume—that is, of course, if you happen to go to one of those flyover states that doesn't have the kind of hunting pressure a lot of us are used to, but we will get to that.

Nearly a decade later, I'm gearing up for another season with a heavy emphasis on public land deer, and it has become something else to me. The pursuit of whitetails on open-to-all-ground has moved from a stage where I had something to prove to something I simply enjoy. And you can too.

Here's how.

PUBLIC LAND REALITY

There are a lot of things that make this country special, and near the top of that list, at least in my humble opinion, is our availability of public land.

It comes in many forms, and an awful lot of it is open to hunting. That is something we should all appreciate and fight for, because if we lose that, we lose something we will never get back.

Most of us have access to public land, whether it's in our backyard or a few hours down the road. The quality of it varies quite a bit, but the reality is that nearly all of us at least have a place to hunt. What makes that better is that even the most heavily hunted parcels usually have a few deer roaming around, which means there is always a chance at an animal. If there is one cadre of outdoorsmen and -women who understand optimism, it's bowhunters.

Bowhunters on public land, to be exact.

Understanding what is available to you specifically is the first step to successfully bowhunting it. This is trickier than it sounds on the surface, largely because so many of us have our minds made up about public ground. That means that we already believe the land we have access to is either good or bad, worth hunting or not. Most of the time, we believe more negatives about it than positives.

This is the first mistake.

Now, I'll say that there is a lot of heavily hunted ground out there that is very, very difficult to fill tags on. That's the reality in many places, especially anything located close to metropolitan areas. I live 45 minutes north of the Twin Cities, which means I've got roughly one million people in my backyard. Of those, plenty of them bowhunt. Public land around my house is a tough proposition. Not impossible, but very tough.

There are bowhunters in every state who understand what I'm saying. If you don't, consider yourself lucky to live in an area with quality public opportunities close at hand. Most of us, for one reason or another, simply don't have them.

We do, however, have a chance to hunt, and that is definitely not nothing. A lot of us also have better odds of filling tags than we probably believe, often on ground we are ready to write off as worthless. For example, there is a tract of land 10 minutes from my house that is open to public hunting. It's good-sized at a shade over 500 acres, but it gets pounded. Absolutely pounded.

Killing any deer in Cedar Creek Conservation Area is no joke, but it can be done. These days, when I do hunt there, I hunt any deer. The property is located inside our Metro Deer Management Zone, which means unlimited antlerless tags. It also means when I hunt there, I'm looking for any doe or fawn that happens to offer up a high-odds shot.

Rarely does that happen, but it happens enough to get me to go in there a few times per season and sit. The last deer I killed there, a mature doe that ended up getting spooked by a woodcock hunter and his English Spaniel, stopped right next to my stand in what was a very bad move on her part. It was a crazy hunt that never should have gone my way, but it did.

Cue that optimism thing again.

I also like roaming that property in search of woodcock with my own dog, and what I find each and every fall is that there are bucks in there. Usually there is a young buck living right next to the parking area in a low, swampy spot that most bowhunters walk right past to get to what they believe will be better ground. Then there are other deer that hole up where the woodcock like to feed, and while they aren't pushovers, they are killable. Better than that, they are there for all of us to hunt.

That stated, I wouldn't go in there thinking I was going to arrow a Pope & Young-class buck or nothing, because nothing is what I would get. So would you, because, unfortunately, you can't hunt what isn't there. A lot of hunters don't seem to understand that.

There is a balance to where our individual standards should be set. We need to factor in the deer we have a chance of encountering, along with a litany of personal factors. How good of a hunter are you, really? That matters. How much hunting time do you get each season? How willing are you to get up when the alarm goes off for the fifth morning in a row? The answers to all of these questions (and plenty more) will inform your decision on what deer is good enough for you.

There is also the pesky business of what you actually want to shoot or, more importantly, what caliber of deer you want to hunt. Maybe a forky is good enough, or perhaps you're at the stage where any two-year-old will do just fine. This is highly subjective, but one thing I always tell hunters is that there are only about three people in your life who actually care about the size of deer you kill. One is you. One is probably a trusted hunting partner, and one will be your spouse—and in that case, she's probably lying for your benefit.

Hunt for what makes you happy, and understand how likely it is that a deer of that caliber will walk by at some time during the season. This is relevant to private land hunters but absolute critical for public land bowhunters.

Eventually, after a bit of mind-grinding, plenty of scouting, and probably some actual hunting, you'll settle on the kind of deer you want. Or if you're like me, you'll make your decision as he (or she) walks by. If the heart rate redlines, it's time to shoot. If not, it's time to pass.

I'm a huge fan of this type of in-the-moment decision-making for a few different reasons. First off, before the season opens it's easy to be chock-full of optimism. After a few weekends of dodging the crowds and getting your butt kicked by the deer, that seemingly endless hope can abruptly find its end, and what your standards were only a few weeks earlier might suddenly change.

It's also the painful reality that life gets in the way of hunting season, and while you may have fully intended to hunt four evenings a week, you didn't anticipate sick kids, having to work late, broken-down vehicles, and a host of other curveballs that life can toss your way. Without a decent amount of time to devote to it, bowhunting becomes exponentially more difficult.

Toss in the burnout factor that can creep in with an endeavor as tough as bowhunting for deer on public land, and you'll find that the whitetail you thought would make you happy while daydreaming during the pre-season doesn't exist, but the one browsing his way through while you're on stand does. That might just be the buck (or doe) you should shoot.

If he's small, so be it. If you're worried about the inevitable small-buck shaming that comes with thumping a 43-inch five-pointer, there are a couple of options. First, don't post pictures of it on social media if you don't want to hear anything negative. If you absolutely must see your face-painted, smiling mug on Facebook or Instagram, expect some negative sentiments. Deer hunters are notorious for imposing their values on one another without much consideration for the reality that we are all individuals.

You could, always, just not care what others think, too. That's the best way to go about it. Even though I present my hunting stories to thousands of people through print and digital entities, it's still a strangely personal pursuit for me. I really don't care much what someone thinks of the bucks I arrow because it doesn't involve them. Neither does the decision on what I'll shoot or let walk.

It's worked well for me so far, and it will for you too.

IDENTIFYING BETTER HUNTING GROUND AT HOME
AND ABROAD

Not all land is created equal. Tune in to outdoor programming some evening if you're into a little masochism, and in-between the next husband-and-wife superstar celebrities selling you junk and rednecks with carefully applied face paint engaging in one too many man hugs, you'll see dreamy deer ground. On screen you'll witness slow panning shots of fields and food plots that are littered with whitetails, more whitetails, in fact, than you'll see in a month.

More whitetails, in some cases, than you'll see in an entire season.

That land, which is managed for whitetails, is not what you'll be hunting. No one is going to raise a buck from a milk-mustachioed fawn to a 6.5-year-old giant just so you can tack another head to the wall in your man cave. You will be hunting land where every deer has a target on its side from the moment it loses its spots throughout its first full season and beyond. This environment creates deer that don't put up with a whole lot of mistakes, which is something we will get into later.

For now, your job is to find good land, or at least good-enough land. The best part of this process is that you can start it at home any time of the year you'd like. In fact, I find most of my best public spots during the winter without ever lacing up my boots.

Of course, this involves some serious computer time. I bought a tablet a few years ago simply to make things easier when checking trail cameras, but it has also become my dedicated scouting machine. I spend a crazy amount of time looking at Google Earth and Game and Fish websites in order to take in as much aerial photography as I can. When I find something I like, I take a screenshot of it and it goes right into my folder of images.

Those images are then emailed to me so I can access them via my phone when I'm actually out scouting. For now though, it's all about the aerial photography and what it shows.

Naturally, whitetail hunters tend to look for two things: food and cover. There's nothing wrong with this, but on public land food is secondary to security. Actually, on common dirt everything is secondary to security for the whitetail. Deer are amazing at finding ways to fill their bellies, and even in the late season, they aren't going to allow hunger pangs to put them in danger.

Cover is more important. Much more important. They need places where you and every other hunter won't be able to kill them. This is the kind of cover that tends to look like the perfect spot for a cottontail rabbit hunt. While it's not easy to see on aerial photography, you can zoom in enough to tell the difference between older-growth trees and actual deer-hiding brush and thickets.

While scouring aerial images for deer-friendly cover, pay special attention to access as well. Easy access is the enemy. Always. There are no exceptions to this rule, unfortunately. If someone can walk a mowed trail throughout a specific tract of land, they will. Or, most likely, lots of people. This only gets worse if ATVs, which in many ways have become the go-to method of transportation for lazy hunters, are allowed. If four-wheelers and UTVs are allowed on a parcel of public, I don't hunt it unless it's huge. By huge, I mean hundreds of thousands of acres. Otherwise, no thanks.

Notice I wrote "allowed" on public land. I hunt some properties in northern Wisconsin where ATV use is prohibited by law. What is very clear up there, every time I sit in stand, is that I must be the only one following the law. A few years ago I sat for eight days during the rut on those public parcels and never once had a property to myself without someone cruising through on a quad. It was maddening, and probably the main reason why my enthusiasm for hunting the big woods has waned so much. Keep that in mind when researching public land. Not only will you be dealing with law-abiding hunters, but you'll also encounter the folks who couldn't give a rip about the rules.

I'll put the complaining aside to get back to the task at hand. Take a look at roads on aerial photography and how they relate to your chosen property. If there are several roads throughout, you might want to keep looking. Even one road or two-track can ruin a potentially good spot if it bisects a property and allows for easy access.

The ideal property has limited access and provides an opportunity for you to hike at least a mile. If you are willing to cover a legitimate mile on foot with a stand and a set of sticks strapped to your pack, you'll leave behind nearly all of the competition. Remember, whitetail hunters aren't elk hunters. These days, you'd better not show your face in elk camp or at a western hunting expo unless you're willing to hike seven miles from the trailhead, straight up for 12,000 feet, with an 85-pound pack on your back—just to start your elk hunt.

Things aren't quite as intense in the whitetail woods. One mile is good enough, although there are a few things you should look for that will make that mile a bit trickier, but much more effective.

Hills: It's silly, I know, but the reality is that if you have to climb a hill, you can leave a lot of competition behind. The single-best chunk of public land I've ever found in my life is a section of ground in Nebraska where you can either stay on the level and hunt a creek bottom, or hike up a bluff and hunt the tops of a few ridges. The property gets hunted hard all season long, but I'd be willing to bet that at least 95 percent of the hunters focus their efforts on the creek bottom.

In 2014, a buddy and I set out to hunt that property during the rut. When we arrived, we threw together our camp and then hiked our gear up to the top so we could quickly set up the following morning in the dark. While we were sipping coffee well before sunrise, at least seven or eight vehicles drove in and parked. We watched a steady stream of headlamps bobbing along into the creek bottom. One of them broke off and veered up the hill.

We met the hunter in the dark on top and had a whispered discussion. The bowhunter, a very nice fellow from Michigan who was hunting with his father, mentioned he had a stand that was located three-quarters of the way down the ridge. In other words, he'd be sitting between my buddy and I. We all set out together, with my hunting partner peeling off first.

I wished our new friend good luck when we reached his flagged trail and set out to my own stand tree. It was well before first light when I saw a buck ghost through with his nose to the ground, which usually portends good things to come. As the sun broke across the horizon behind me, I could see a lone doe feeding in a private cornfield.

Then I heard a loud grunt.

In a total rookie, reactionary move I stood straight up as soon as I heard it. Immediately I got busted by a doe at 75 yards, which stung, but not as much as realizing what kind of company she currently kept. A few bucks, all great deer from what I could tell by peering through the cedars, circled her. Even though she had me pegged, those rut-crazed bucks didn't care. They had other things on their minds, and soon enough they were grunting and nosing her.

When their advances got the best of her and she couldn't take it any longer, she trotted past me. I drew and waited for the first boyfriend, who was all of 140 inches. In what can only be described as a classic, buck-fever induced meltdown, I whiffed. I quickly nocked another arrow and waited for the second buck, a solid 120-inch deer. He trotted through so fast that ethically there was nothing to do but watch.

I was bemoaning a lost chance when I heard a deer trotting in my direction and saw a massive rack coming my way. I dialed my sight down, drew, and mouth-bleated to stop him at seven yards, all at the same time. Fortunately, my second arrow of the morning flew much better. When I tried to sit down and collect myself, I couldn't. I had the shakes so bad that I just had to hold onto the pine tree in which I'd placed my stand and ride out the convulsions. I've had a lot of amazing encounters in the deer woods, but I don't remember a single time where I was shaking as bad as I was after that buck took off.

When I regained some base level of body and brain function, I texted my buddy to let him know that I'd shot a great deer. He returned the text with good news of his own, saying that he'd shot a young eight-pointer.

We retrieved my buck first. I reckoned the deer at a solid 140 inches, but he grew the more we looked at him. The 10-pointer, with serious mass and some palmation on both of his main beams, ended up grossing 156 inches. My buddy's buck ended up requiring a serious tracking job, but when we did find him he was nearly at camp, which made the drag much easier.

As we were discussing our good fortune, our Michigan friend strolled into our camp and said that he'd arrowed a deer as well. The buck, a 17-inch-wide eight-pointer, was a beautiful deer, and he was a very happy hunter.

If you're keeping track, that's three bucks off of the same ridge, on public land, during the same morning, while at least 10 other hunters were sitting below us. I never saw anyone else take a deer out of that property, but we had tripled up partially because we'd been willing to climb a good-sized hill.

These days, if I can find a public spot that requires a serious climb right off the bat, that's going to get my attention. No one wants to carry a stand up a big hill, but I'll do it. I've seen the results of doing it multiple times.

Rivers: You might not have to go vertical to get a buck—you might just have to get a little wet.

While digitally scouting potential public hotspots, keep an eye out for moving water. Rivers and streams are goldmines for bowhunters. First off, they tend to provide killer access. If you can wade to your treestand, you can usually avoid being smelled, heard, or seen by the local ungulates. Just how crucial that is can't be overstated.

It is important to note that just because you can wade into a river in your home state and legally hike up or down its length, that's not the case everywhere. Navigable water laws vary a lot by state and even throughout individual states depending on what type of land they wind through. In some states, any navigable water is considered a public highway, and you can walk in it or on the banks up to the high-water mark while staying on the right side of the law. In others, you might be breaking the law by setting foot on the river bottom depending on who owns the land and water rights. This is important information to keep in mind before you plan to build a river into your hunting strategy.

My favorite type of river is large enough to have high banks for better concealment, but not so large that I risk getting swept away or stepping into a deep hole in the dark. This size of river will tend to have some amazing whitetail crossings, because there will be certain spots where it's much easier for them to go from bank to bank. They don't want to swim if they don't have to, so they'll find shallow areas that allow for easy walking. These types of crossings are often good all season, and if they can be accessed by a little wading, you are well on your way to excellent hunting.

River crossings are some of the travel corridors easiest to identify via aerial photography as well. Take a look at the surrounding terrain, and you'll likely see features that funnel movement to a specific spot. Better yet, you can usually zoom in and see rapids or at least rocks periscoping out of the river's surface. These spots, most likely, are shallow enough to cross.

If for some reason you can't see the surface well enough to pick out a few spots where deer might cross, don't fret. You are going to have to get wet anyway, so you might as well lace up a pair of old boots and start sloshing your way upstream. Make note of all crossings and any nearby trees that might be worth setting up in. Pay attention to the orientation of the river, and think about wind direction at each potential stand site. The best setup is one in which you can sit where the wind will blow over or down the river, well away from the likeliest crossing.

Rivers and streams aren't only good for crossing setups and access, however. They also tend to be framed in the best cover around. This is true everywhere, but especially if you hunt west of the Mississippi. And the farther west you go, the better this gets for a couple of reasons.

The first is that things tend to get drier in the Plains States, which means that you're more likely to encounter quality whitetail cover and browse near a good water source. It also means that the land, at least right next to the river, won't be farmed. This is a general rule, of course, but ground on each side of a waterway should have some cover left along it even if it's only a thin strip that is punctuated by a few cottonwoods.

This also means that creek bottoms are more likely to be public than the prime land that can be farmed half a mile away. There is nothing I like more than finding a thick, nasty river bottom that is framed on both sides by private food sources. Locate that, and you'll locate a bedding area, staging area, and a hunting spot that won't likely get pounded by every weekend warrior out there because access usually takes some work.

Although I've only briefly touched on safety, it's worth saying again: be careful if you're going to wade anywhere, especially if you're going to do it in the dark. And pay attention to the river conditions. Flooding in the fall happens, and some waterway that you usually can cross without getting your knees wet might suddenly be two feet deeper and a totally different animal after some upstream storms.

I ran into this in 2014 while bowhunting in North Dakota. Usually the Little Missouri River is low and very easy to cross in most spots around the areas I hunt, but that year the water was up. Way up.

I glassed during the days leading up to the opener to see what the deer were doing, and it became pretty clear that they were either on one side or the other. The problem was that most of them were on the other side. I only found one small bachelor group on my side. Try as I might—and believe me, I tried—I couldn't find a safe way to wade across. I contemplated trying to buy a kayak somewhere, but that was a long shot and a desperation move.

I ended up focusing on the bucks that were stuck on my side. Since they had limited options, they were way easier to hunt than I expected. The buck that I arrowed on opening night out of the group was a beautiful, full-velvet eight-pointer that followed his buddies through the same pinch-point I had watched them slip through the previous night. He wasn't as big as some of the deer across the river, but I didn't risk drowning to get to him.

Be careful when you're dealing with unfamiliar water.

Food and Water: There are other things worth investigating from a digital, bird's-eye view as well. For example, some public land will have plenty of food sources. Some, like certain tracts of public land located in northern Missouri or parts of Oklahoma, will even feature state-planted food plots. This is awesome to see, but in my experience, it's also a magnet for bowhunting pressure. Other parcels of public will feature fields that are leased to local farmers, which means that the deer theoretically have all they need on public and therefore won't need to travel long distances to reach food or bedding cover on private.

Focus on food sources if you must, but remember that they are where most of the hunting pressure will be concentrated. If you want to sit over something that will draw deer, it's a much better bet to try to locate a small pond that is tucked well off of the easiest stuff. Deer drink every day, and they are much more likely to visit a small waterhole during shooting hours than they are a field edge where they know two-legged predators await their arrival.

Ponds and other small water sources are season-long activity producers, and as an added bonus, are highly visible on aerial photography. If you need a reliable spot, they're it. If you're planning to travel across state lines to hunt a new property, you could do a lot worse than planning to sit a secluded pond. Trust me.

While perusing your potential hunting spots with a pond or other water-source ambush plan in mind, try to pick out individual stand trees or blind sites and approach routes. Often, ponds will be tucked into drainages that aren't as thick with trees as a full-on forest. This means you should be able to zoom in and see individual trees. You won't be able to tell with 100 percent certainty whether they are good for a stand, but you can get pretty close.

If you don't see any trees that look remotely like they'll accommodate an aerial approach, then you can plan to haul in a blind or build a natural blind once you get there. Remember, too, that on some aerial photography sites you can scroll through various images to see the spot during different parts of the year. Identifying the best stand trees is easiest when there is no foliage on the trees, and you might be able to scroll back in time through various images to see a late-winter or early-spring snapshot of your spot. In that image, you'll be able to see what you really need to see when it comes to a specific tree.

This can save you a lot of time and headaches when it comes time to go in and set up, or actually hunt, a given spot.

3

THE SWEET SMELL OF BURNING BOOT LEATHER

Now that you've pinned down a few potential hotspots, you'll need to get in there and take a good look around. Several, in fact. Aerial photography provides an excellent opportunity to easily get to know the layout of a property, but you can't know what's really there until you see it for yourself.

Scouting, actual old-fashioned scouting, has been largely replaced by trail cameras in this modern age of hunting. That may seem like a fair tradeoff, but it's not. Trail cameras will not tell you what's really going on in the woods. They may provide a snapshot of activity in a particular area, but you can bet that they are missing the bigger picture. When you really break it down, cameras are only covering a tiny fraction of the woods.

This reality, which personally has been hard to stomach, was driven home a few years ago while I sat on stand during Minnesota's opening weekend. I had a camera strapped to a tree maybe five yards from my stand. Throughout the night I had three little bucks and several does cruise through. Two of the bucks squared up a few times and gave it their all, to the point where the larger of the two actually knocked his rival ass-over-apple-cart, which was something I had never witnessed before.

The youngsters fought their way completely around my tree, and thus, completely around my camera. In total, I saw nine deer during that sit and know for a fact that most of them walked by my trail camera. At the end of the night I had a single picture of one of the bucks in what was a total disappointment of a memory-card check.

Now, cameras have gotten better in the past few years, and it goes without saying the latest iteration would have most likely captured more images. I don't care. I want to see deer doing their thing, and I want to find sign of their comings and goings. I don't care about getting a picture of them anymore, unless I'm working a really small property. Otherwise, it's boots on the ground for this guy. Always.

If you absolutely must use trail cameras, use them wisely. We have a tendency to set them where we know we'll get lots of images—like, for example, on the edge of an agricultural field or a food plot. Sure, this is a good place to get images, but what are you really going to learn? Not much.

On public land, this is also a great way to donate your camera to unscrupulous individuals who would gladly steal them. A better trail-camera strategy is to hang them where you don't know what is going on. I like to use them to monitor trails in the thick stuff where you can't observe deer activity through optics. Use your cameras to answer questions, not just reaffirm what you already know.

And if you're worried about your expensive digital scouter walking away, do what I do. I carry a single section of climbing sticks and use a trail-camera mount. If I find a spot that asks a question a camera might answer, I mount a camera 10 feet off the ground and pull my sticks when I leave. I get *a lot* of pictures of people walking by who never look up, as well as plenty of photos of deer cruising through. Just remember to bring your sticks when you return to check your camera; otherwise, you won't be able to retrieve it unless you've got a 75-inch vertical and are extremely coordinated.

Whether you're hiking or hanging cameras, "deer scouting" is a general term which can cover a variety of different ways to figure out the movements of local ungulates. Of particular relevance to this chapter are the types of scouting you should engage in for the eight or nine months of the off-season.

Winter Scouting: I'm of the humble opinion that nothing is more valuable than time spent in the woods from January to end of March. This time, which is usually devoted to shed hunting, is the period in which you can walk every inch of your chosen hunting ground (or a potential new spot) without any fear of spooking deer or educating them in any meaningful manner. Better yet, or at least just as good, is the fact that the woods are as bare as they are going to be all year, which really allows you to read the terrain.

If you're in the North Country like I am, winter scouting might mean waiting until March or even early April to get out there depending on the snowpack. You can scout any time no matter the depth of the snow, but there is a diminished return when you're slogging through three feet of powder trying to figure out what the bucks were doing last October.

Some years, however, the snow won't be an issue. The key, no matter when you get out there, is to look for last year's sign. Trails and rubs are the most important, although you may see some scrapes as well if the ground is bare.

What I tend to look for are trails in the thick stuff. This is public land, remember, so the movement in the security cover is what you should care about the most. In my immediate neck of the woods, that means cattail sloughs, alder thickets, and other places that simply suck to walk through.

Trails alone aren't enough, however.

I want to see trails that are marked with rubs. Good-sized rubs are preferable, but any rubs will do. I've watched mature bucks make rubs that most would credit to 40-inch six-pointers, but I've never seen a dink make a big rub. Either way, rubs are good. Very good. Any trail that leads through security cover that sports some rubs is worth investigating. If you find this during a winter-scouting foray, keep an eye out for a stand tree because you'll probably need it.

Also, take a long look at how any of these in-the-thick trails work their way through the terrain. You might see that while they seem to randomly cross a cattail slough, they actually connect a couple of opposing points of high ground. Or you might find a trail that snakes its way well downwind of the nearest destination food source.

When you watch deer move through the woods, it may appear as if they are randomly meandering their way along. They probably are not. Randomness isn't all that common in nature, especially in prey animals. They tend to cover ground with a purpose, although whatever that may be might not be evident to us.

While cruising public land on winter-scouting missions, mark up a map or drop waypoints on your phone or GPS unit. These days I tend to go to my mapping feature and drop a pin on my hotspots right on my smartphone. Then I take a screenshot so I have it in my images folder as well. This step, while it might seem like overkill, is not. Remembering where you found the perfect ambush trees seems easy enough when you're staring at the tree, but three months later it won't be. If legal, you might be able to flag a trail or a specific tree with biodegradable flagging tape as well.

Naturally, you can tie in some antler hunting on these walks, but don't get so focused on collecting bone that you miss the big picture. If you do find a shed, that's a bonus and a clue to who survived last hunting season.

This happened to me several years ago. Through winter scouting I found a spot on public land in Minnesota that was covered in thigh-sized rubs. It looked as if a giant had staged on a ridge right next to a swamp, and I decided I should try to figure out if that was true. That spring, after extensive shed hunting, my golden retriever stopped to paw something in the yellow saw grass. It looked like a tine, only too big. When she tried to pry the antler from the matted grass I found myself looking at the biggest shed of my life, which had fallen not 200 yards from the best concentration of sign.

I never matched that shed up, but I did sneak in during the summer and get a look at its owner and a couple of his buddies. But before I get into the pursuit of that deer, I should mention this: winter scouting isn't just about deer sign. You need to look for hunter sign as well.

If I find an area that gets my Spidey senses tingling, but I also find someone's treestand or evidence of a stand, I usually forget it. The exception to this is on properties where I find hunter sign everywhere. One of my Nebraska spots is incredible for deer hunting but gets hunted enough where I rarely set a stand in a tree that hasn't already been trimmed by someone else.

That evidence might be from a season before or a decade previously, but it's there. Or I'll peek up through the branches and see an old bow hook screwed into the tree. If a property is good enough, I don't care about past evidence of hunters. If it's so-so, like a lot of my Minnesota and Wisconsin spots, I'll keep looking.

Keep this in mind as the spring threatens to kick in and turkey season is just around the corner. In fact, you might want to consider a combination trip where you try to arrow a gobbler (or shoot one in the face with a 12-gauge, if that's your thing) while roaming public land in search of deer sign. This is my go-to method for scouting out of state. It's easier to justify the road time when there is something more than just scouting out there.

I've turkey hunted Iowa, Missouri, Wisconsin, South Dakota, Iowa, and Nebraska in an attempt to scout land that I was considering making a deer hunting trip to. Some of the trips involved killing turkeys, but all of them involved deciding whether those states would get my hard-earned, nonresident money come fall.

Whether you're turkey hunting and scouting, simply taking a walk through some potential deer ground, or have devoted a long weekend to scouring every inch of your chosen property, remember to keep an eye out for soft edges as well. These can be a little difficult to find when the woods are bare in the late winter, but if you know what you're looking for you'll be able to identify them.

Deer are edge lovers. They just are. They love hard edges, where some kind of well-defined cover meets another kind of well-defined cover. Think of a patch of hardwoods that borders pine trees. Hard edges can also be as simple as a woodline along a field.

But soft edges are different.

A soft edge might be where a three-year-old clear cut meets a five-year-old clear cut. It might be where a one-acre patch of dogwood meets an older-growth coniferous forest. In some cases, it might be where there was a homestead that is long abandoned now and is currently being reclaimed by Mother Nature. Soft edges are often the places that deer either travel along, like an old fence line in the woods, or where they congregate to browse (or, to put it another way, stage).

These are the kinds of places most public land bowhunters will miss or ignore in favor of more obvious locations. They may not be littered with obvious sign, because there might not be any one small spot where the deer spend most of their time.

Oftentimes while winter scouting, I'll walk into the woods off of a food source, and while I'm looking for signs of deer staging the previous fall, I will either jump deer bedded or find several beds in relatively close proximity to one another. If I look really closely, there tends to be a subtle change in the type of cover where the deer seem to feel a little more secure.

Now, in the winter they'll bed on the inside of those soft edges, but they probably won't come fall. They will use them to stage, and that is something that you can bank away and eventually build into a hunting strategy. Lastly, remember that a soft edge usually won't look like much in February, but it certainly will in September when the brush is fully leafed out. Because of that, you might have to use your imagination to really grasp why the deer are using an area where two types of similar-but-different cover meet.

Summer Scouting: Most summer scouting, aside from the trail-camera variety, involves glassing from the comfort of your truck cab while country music plays from the radio and velvet bucks munch on soybeans half a mile away. Aside from a few western state opportunities, this type of scouting is mostly a private land affair.

If you're in the Midwest, South, or East, you aren't all that likely to locate an easy-to-watch, close-to-any-road bachelor group. It's just not going to happen. You'll have to work to find glassing opportunities that the average weekend warrior will miss or simply won't dig into because it's too much work.

The previously mentioned public land giant who was generous enough to leave a massive five-point side where my dog and I would find it was living in some backyards but feeding in a rye field on public. The problem was there was only one way to get into position to glass him without blowing most of the herd out.

The route necessitated going the long way around and then through mosquito-filled woods to climb a ridge that overlooked the field. It also allowed for the chance to play the wind, not only while sitting to glass, but also while sneaking in and out. It wasn't much fun, but the first time I did it, I didn't have to wait long to see what I wanted to see.

The buck, one of the few legitimate Booners I've ever laid eyes on, walked out first. His buddy was a no-slouch 140-inch deer, the kind of buck most of us will never shoot on public land and probably never see, but the big boy was something special. They fed below me for a short time before slipping back into the woods in which he'd left his calling card scarred all over the cedars the previous fall. Later that evening, a great nine-pointer fed into the field. He was still there when I snuck out.

I don't know what happened to the big bucks. They disappeared on me. I snuck into that glassing spot a lot—too much probably—but I never laid eyes on them again. I did see the nine-pointer and several other bucks, but not the two largest. Eventually, I found a salt block with a camera over it close to the trail they used, which might have been the reason for them vanishing into thin air.

As unfortunate as that was, the main point is that you'll have to work to figure out how to observe summertime bucks on Uncle Sam's ground, but it will be worth the extra effort. Any time you can observe any deer, including mature bucks, you're learning.

That's a good thing, the value of which can't be overstated. Watching a buck lazily navigate his way through the landscape can give you so many clues to his habits, and to those of other bucks. If a deer follows a woodline and then drops down into a pond for a drink before setting out across a CRP field to visit some private land groceries, he has provided you with so much information that you can use to set up on him or one of his buddies.

Here's why. If you see a buck do something today, he might not do it tomorrow or within the next week. That's okay, because some other buck might. Or you might not see a deer take the same route again until November when they are on their feet and actively cruising for does. But the main point is, the chance to observe any buck traveling, browsing, feeding, and doing what he does without any influence besides his own whims is a gift. Watch him, watch where he goes, and try to imagine how you'll ambush him when he takes the same route during the season.

If you're new to the summer-glassing game you'll need a few things. Binoculars and a spotting scope are obvious necessities, but don't scrimp on the tripod for your spotting scope. A crappy tripod is a liability and not worth saving $50. Buy a good tripod—you won't regret it. In fact, a quality tripod can make marginal-quality optics good enough for most whitetail applications, while a junk tripod can seriously degrade the usefulness of high-end optics.

I also tend to camo up completely, so a lightweight set of camouflage is a must. A Thermacell unit is another must. I won't scout without one because where I live, mosquitoes are a part of life. A horrible, stupid, constant-annoyance part of life. I've yet to use any kind of insect repellent that functions as well to keep the aerial bloodsuckers at bay as well as a Thermacell unit does.

Buy one (or three) and use it summer scouting, early-season hunting, turkey hunting, fishing off the dock with the kids, or wherever mosquitoes threaten your outdoor enjoyment. They don't pay me a dime, so this recommendation comes straight from a place of experience and nothing else. Few things have changed the way I scout, hunt, and fish more than a Thermacell. I'd sooner forget my spotting scope than my Thermacell when trying to lay eyes on a velvet bruiser.

Gear up correctly and plan to tie in a winter-scouting plan with some summer-glassing forays. Mix in trail-camera use to answer mysteries that would be nearly impossible to solve without them, and you'll be well ahead of your competition by the time the season arrives.

4

SETTING REALISTIC GOALS

I'm of the opinion that one of the main benefits of trail cameras is that they allow us to take inventory of the deer. This is easy enough in the summer on a food source or a mineral site (where legal). This can also be conducted on a water source if you've got access to the right one. If cameras are legal to use on your chosen public spot, this isn't a bad way to use them as long as you're mixing in some other scouting.

When camera images are paired with actual summertime observations, you can make an educated guess on the caliber of deer you're likely to encounter when season opens up.

This is important because too many of us fall prey to the false god of monster bucks. We are inundated with images and videos in outdoor media where 200-inch deer seem common. They're not. Neither are 170-inch deer, or 140-inch deer in most places. Even in the best whitetail states, running into a legit 140-inch deer on public land isn't easy.

It isn't even close.

It isn't impossible either. But it depends on so many different variables that it's a fool's errand to make blanket statements about one state versus the next, or one property versus another. You've got to figure out what is available to you in your spot, because nothing else matters.

This is a process that allows us to set realistic goals about deer hunting, but availability of certain bucks is only part of it. Let's say, for example, that I'm dead set on arrowing a buck on public land in northern Wisconsin. I know from experience that I'm going to be dealing with low deer numbers there, which obviously translates to low buck numbers.

I know that one bad winter can adversely affect the herd for years, and that happens often enough to mean Mother Nature's most recent wrath needs to be accounted for each season. I also know that there are coyotes, bobcats, bears, and wolves there—all of which love eating venison as much as I do. Probably more.

To make matters even more bleak, I also know that there are a lot of hunters and Wisconsin is a two-buck state, meaning hunters can shoot a buck with archery gear and then another one with a firearm. All of this adds up to a somewhat dismal reality that doesn't lend itself to overly picky hunts or to being in any real danger of seeing too many deer on any one sit.

There are, however, also plenty of alder thickets, cranberry bogs, and nasty, no-fun-to-slog-through swamps. These are all sanctuaries, as are the heaven-sent, five-year-old clear cuts that virtually eliminate any effectiveness of deer drives during gun season.

This tips the odds a bit in favor of someone who holds out hope of running into a good buck, because the right cover can go a long way toward allowing a buck to celebrate enough birthdays to be mature, even if he has to spend his entire life dodging a variety of four- and two-legged predators.

In fact, in the area where I hunt in Wisconsin, theoretically the bucks should be genetically inferior to, say, the bucks in northern Iowa, but that doesn't really seem to be the case. The biggest seem to get as big as anywhere—they just aren't as likely to get there before they end up in a predator's stomach or a hunter's chest freezer.

All of that said, I still need to take things further. Even though the area of northern Wisconsin is only a shade under 2.5 hours from my house, that's far enough where I'm not going to drive it for a single sit or even a day of hunting. I much prefer a couple of days stacked together, which means my entire amount of time to hunt there might add up to a week for the whole season. That's not a lot of time to kill a good buck on public land.

Because of that, I refine what I consider to be a good buck. To me, a 2.5-year-old on public land there is a hell of a trophy, and any buck that age or older that happens to pass my stand would be wise to do so on a dead run. Anything older than a 2.5-year-old, and we are talking about something pretty special that is not only likely to catch my attention, but could end up at my taxidermist even though he might not boast an impressive score.

These kinds of evolving (or devolving) standards travel with me to other states as well. If I've only got a few days to hunt a different state, I might go on an any-buck mission depending on the timing of the hunt. If it's a rut hunt in a decent state, I might let some youngsters pass. If it's the beginning of October and I've got three days to fill a tag, those same youngsters better steer clear of me.

While I get that everyone wants to arrow 150-inch bucks each year, that's just not reality. If you decide to set your standards according to the deer available, the time you have and are willing to put in, and, lastly, what will make you happy, then you'll have a hell of a lot more fun deer hunting.

I learn this every few years when my standards get out of whack and I decide I'm something pretty special in the deer woods. My latest lesson occurred while I was sitting in a treestand in North Dakota. The morning sun was already causing the early-September temperatures to rise to uncomfortable levels when I saw a wide, velvet rack bobbing its way through the weeds. I'd seen the eight-point buck while scouting and knew that I'd be really happy to wrap my tag around his antlers.

When he entered my shooting lane, that's pretty much what I figured was going to happen. Instead, I whiffed. Badly. The deer bounded a few steps and looked around, which gave me enough time to nock another arrow, compose myself, and whiff again. As he hotfooted it across the river I watched what I assumed was my one good chance for the trip run out of my life, completely unscathed.

The thing I remember most, besides having fully delaminated on a great buck, was watching him bound away across the river and just how wide his rack looked from that angle. I figured him at close to 20 inches inside spread, and that running-away view made it look like about 25. It was one of those, "I'm not crying; I just have some dust in my eyes" moments that all of us bowhunters will eventually experience.

Things got worse from there as the deer made wide circles around my stand. Originally, I thought I'd have a solid chance of arrowing a 125-inch buck in my four-day hunt, and truth be told, I did. I just blew it. And because I blew it, I found myself having a lot less fun than I should have.

It was to the point that I walked to that stand for the last evening in a sour mood. My pity party was in full swing when I climbed in and started to hoist my bow up. That's when the ground moved and a five-foot rattlesnake reared back to strike. I had to have been standing right next to him without even noticing. Missing a good buck twice suddenly didn't seem like the end of the world.

I watched that snake slither away, and then I settled into the stand. When the sun connected with the horizon, a calm settled over the river bottom and a strange sense of peace took over me. I realized that I wasn't going to kill a buck, but I didn't care. Sitting in that cottonwood watching a few random ducks paddle by was a heck of a lot better than most things I could have been doing. I was so zoned out in my appreciation for the land around me that I failed to notice the young eight-pointer walking right at me.

When he was 15 yards away I realized that I had about three seconds to shoot or he would be out of my life. The buck heard me draw but instead of bolting, he made the mistake of stopping broadside. That deer, which might measure 75 inches, is still one of my favorite deer of my career because of how I came to get him. I've killed deer twice as big that don't mean nearly as much to me as he does.

There have been others like that as well, many others in fact. All of them involved a lot of hard work, some luck, and the backdrop of expectations that didn't exceed what reality was most likely to offer up for me. In fact, what I find in my life is that my range of public land bucks is a wide one, and while I'm always more excited to kill a 150-inch buck than a 50-inch buck, by the time the next season has rolled around I think back on both with an equal level of fondness. And when I'm bacon-wrapping some steaks for the grill during a random evening in the summer, I tend to look at that 50-incher with a *little* more fondness than his bigger brother, because a medium-rare backstrap off of a young buck is a thing of beauty in and of itself.

5

PUBLIC LAND EQUIPMENT ESSENTIALS

The thing about hunting public land and finding any level of success is that it's a commitment on all fronts. That means the work ethic, of course, but also the equipment. Gear choice matters, and some of the better (read: more expensive) stuff is a necessary evil.

For instance, because I hunt throughout the season, from opening weekend where it might be 80 degrees to the last bitter days of December when we might not see a positive temperature reading all day in my home state, I realize that what clothing I wear is often the most important decision I make.

Quality clothing isn't cheap, but it's worth it. Being too hot or too cold or wearing a jacket that is too bulky to draw your bow are the realities of subpar clothing. These days, I'd rather have a cheap bow and an expensive camouflage suit designed for my hunting conditions than the latest flagship bow and camo from Wally World.

Now, on a nice October afternoon sit you might not feel like you need the best duds out there, because you don't. But if you have to hike a mile into your stand when it's 60 degrees and sit while the temps drop into the 40s, you might. And if you're going to hunt extreme temperatures at either end of the spectrum, the best clothing is always a plus.

Because I pack in quite a bit, I'm to the point now where I tend to opt for western clothing. If it's designed to work well while you hike the mountains in search of bugling elk, it'll be ideal for early-season, go-deep public land whitetail hunts.

For cold-weather hunts, the right base layers and outer layers are a must as well. This is where some of the dedicated late-season apparel really holds its own. Base layers of merino wool covered in a couple of layers of insulating clothing and then an outer shell that truly blocks the wind are crucial. And don't worry about being a little bit wussy about cold weather. These days, I am. I've got an addiction to hand warmers that is unlikely to be cured any time soon. I've got nothing left to prove in the treestand and would rather be comfortable than manly.

One thing to consider if you really need to bulk up to stay warm is articulation. I hate vests in most of my life. You would never, ever, ever catch me wearing one in any situation—except for late-season hunting. I love vests that are stuffed with the right insulation because they keep my core warm and allow my arms to move. This matters not only while drawing a bow, but also while climbing into and out of your stand.

Stands, Sticks, and Safety Gear: If you've got clothing covered, you'll need to consider treestands and climbing sticks. I'd say about half of the public land I hunt is regulated in such a way that you can't leave stands out overnight or that they can only be left out for a short time. It's frustrating, but it's not likely to change any time soon.

Because of this, lightweight stands are a must. I see hang-on treestands that weigh in excess of 20 pounds, and I throw up just a little in my mouth each time. If you're getting a cushy hang-on stand for private ground where you can drive an ATV up to your tree and set it up leisurely in the summer, go for it.

For hunting public? Forget it.

Small and lightweight are two adjectives that describe every stand I use. Currently, my stands average about 8.5 pounds apiece, which is feathery lightweight. I can strap a stand like that to my pack, along with sticks, and not destroy my back muscles while hiking in, and I can carry them quietly.

As far as sticks go, if you go cheap you'll regret it. I like sticks that marry together tightly, weigh at most three pounds apiece, and attach firmly and easily to the tree. Cheap sticks tend to be heavier and, quite frankly, less safe. I had a section pull off of a tree on me one time in Wisconsin that sent me on an unintentional bungee jump with my lifeline, which is a puckery moment, believe me.

The reason the sticks pulled off was that the strap connection was junk. Cheap junk with a horrible design. I've since retired those steps but still see that style in the woods quite a bit, and I cringe every time I do. If I hadn't been using a lifeline when mine pulled off of the tree, I'd have fallen maybe 10 feet. It probably wouldn't have killed me, but it probably wouldn't have done me a whole lot of good either. These days, it's expensive well-made steps or nothing.

The good news is that if you're setting up and taking down stands a lot, you don't need to fill your garage with 40 sets. I get by with about three or four, because they rarely spend more than one night in the woods. It really is a matter of quality over quantity.

It goes without saying, although I'll say it anyway, that I always use a safety harness. My current harness weighs 2.5 pounds and is streamlined, quiet, and, as I've found out, excellent at keeping me from swan diving to the frozen earth. With that harness, I use a lineman's belt when setting up and taking down every stand. If you don't use a good harness with a lineman's belt, you are missing out. Trust me. They allow for hands-free setup and take down, which is most welcome.

This might sound like enough safety gear, but I'm not done yet. Use a lifeline too. If you're going to go up and down a tree more than once, you should be using a lifeline. They are cheap insurance against the cold, hard fact that most of us fall when we are climbing in or climbing out of a stand. This may sound like a lot of stuff to carry, but it's not. It doesn't even add up in weight to that of a decent pack for elk hunting (and you won't have to climb mountains for whitetails, probably).

Of course, you can also opt for a climbing stand and skip the sticks and the lifeline. I use a climber sparingly, mostly because I just don't find enough trees to use them in. On some of my private spots, I've got trees that I know will perfectly accommodate a climber, but on public I tend to stay away from them. If you have the option, they can be an excellent choice provided you scout out not only killer spots, but killer spots with tall, limb-free tree trunks. It can be done, but it isn't always the most efficient way.

One type of spot where I do find a fair amount of trees that are perfect for climbing stands is on land that was selectively logged. In some of the big-timber areas of our country where the paper industry is alive and well, you can find public land where logging operations will take out most of the trees but leave some seed trees.

I've got 80 acres in northern Wisconsin on a property like this that I'm awfully fond of. Through scouting and hunting I know I can walk along a number of old logging roads to reach multiple trees that are ideal for climbing stands. As an added bonus, most of the deer seem to like to use the logging roads too, so it's almost like having shooting lanes cut for you. If you look hard enough, you'll probably find some public land that offers just the right trees in a good-enough spot.

Pack Essentials: There are other things I wouldn't want to live without. Several lights come to mind. I always carry a headlamp, and then a backup with spare batteries. Losing a morning hunt because you can't find your way to your stand is a total waste of hunting time, and as we all eventually come to find out, the absolute definition of frustrating.

And it's so preventable.

Good headlamps also allow for blood trailing and, hopefully, field dressing in the dark. The more quality gear you have with you, the better you'll engage in recovery efforts and the fewer headaches you'll have. Don't skimp on lighting.

I also always carry biodegradable flagging tape, reflective tacks, and a simple tow rope for my bow. I don't know what amazes me the most about the world of tow ropes. It's either that the industry keeps figuring out new ways to sell them to us or that we find reasons to buy anything other than a simple rope. Either way, I'm a firm believer in simplicity and function, and nothing is more simple and functional for hauling up and lowering a bow than a 20-foot rope.

I don't want metal or plastic clips, retractable devices, or anything unnecessary on my tow rope. I also don't want a 30-foot rope when a 20-footer would do, or a tangled-all-the-frickin'-time rope. I spent one season with a rope that would knot up as soon as I touched it, and I grew to hate it. For some reason, I kept using it. By the end of the season I felt the rope and I were in an abusive relationship, and it was intentionally doing a crappy job of being a tow rope just to tick me off. It took me longer than it should to ball that malicious prick up and throw it in the trash. So, yeah, I'm picky about my ropes, and while they don't make or break a hunt, they can degrade just a little of the enjoyment. Why risk it?

I also always keep a saw and pruners in my truck, but not in my pack. The reason for this is that on an awful lot of public land, it's illegal to trim anything. If I have one gripe about the laws governing bowhunting public ground, it's that. I realize allowing hunters to trim would lead to zipperheads going into the woods and cutting huge shooting lanes, so I understand where the laws come from. But still, not being able to trim sucks and requires extra-special attention when eyeballing potential stand trees.

A couple things that I never leave in my truck are a knife that is honed to a razor's edge, a spare release aid, and my camera gear. Binoculars are a must as well, although magnification depends on personal preference. For me, that tends to be either 8x32s or 10x40s. I prefer the larger binoculars as long as they aren't too heavy (usually they aren't). In addition to binoculars, I've always got an angle-compensating rangefinder, which I use a lot because I shoot with single-pin adjustable sights quite a bit.

I like to know my exact range whenever I can. If a buck is at 27 yards, and I have time to confirm that with my rangefinder, I do just that and then dial in to exactly 27. I've tried the oft-touted method of ranging random objects as soon as you sit down and then committing them to memory so when a deer passes, you can just conjure up the range of the nearest landmark. The problem with that strategy for me is that I use to drink a lot, so my memory isn't all that sharp and I tend to forget how far away a certain stump is as soon as I've ranged it. Naturally, if a deer comes in under 20 yards I don't range it because I don't need to. Anything much farther and you can bet I'll be popping a reading off of his side if it's at all feasible to do.

I feel this is a must for most of us. Knowing the exact range is a crucial factor in making the shot. This is Shooting 101 stuff, but I don't know how often I hear someone say they missed a deer because they used the wrong pin after estimating the distance incorrectly.

If you can know, you should know.

Scent Control: Whether I'm doing a seminar or it's through email, the question I get asked most often by bowhunters involves my methods for scent control. This is a tricky one, so stick with me.

First off, there is no substitute for playing the wind. If you want to make your life as a hunter easy, play the wind always. I have access to every scent-control product on the market, and I still plan every sit around the wind. To give me the best advantage possible, I've become reliant on ScoutLook, which is a hunting-related weather app you can download for free. It's good for weather, but it's also good for seeing where the wind is going to be blowing in very specific spots, like those where your treestands are located. I don't know how often I check ScoutLook throughout the season, but it's a lot.

Playing the wind isn't always an option, however. When I'm on the road trying to arrow a river-bottom buck in just a few days' time, I sometimes have to push it wind-wise because I've only got a few setups. At this point, where legal, I use an Ozonics unit. There is a lot of misinformation about ozone and whether it can actually work for hunters. It can, but you have to understand how.

Ozone is a bleaching agent that occurs naturally in the environment. You know how right after a thunderstorm the air smells clean? That's because lightning has fractured oxygen molecules and created ozone. You can smell it because it's heavier than the atmosphere, meaning it sinks toward the ground. An active ozone generator creates a constant stream of ozone, which is unstable and seeks to bond to other molecules, like those stinky bacterial molecules we create on our skin. It sounds like science fiction, but we've been using ozone since the late 1800s to purify water and air. It's proven, and it works.

Now, it doesn't work perfectly. Deer sometimes smell you even when you've got an Ozonics unit running, but they don't usually freak out. They tend to stick their noses in the air, look around for a while, and then walk away. I much prefer that type of reaction to them stomping and snorting wildly before booking it through the woods.

When I first received an original Ozonics unit, I thought it was complete bunk. I set out to prove just that on some public land near my house. The first night I hunted with it, I could hear the little fan running overhead while I sat tucked beneath a cedar tree on the ground.

The first does to approach went straight downwind of me at maybe 20 yards. They walked right past and out into the field in front of me. I assumed the wind was doing something funky, and they'd simply missed my scent stream. I was getting ready to shoot one of them when I heard the little fan shut off as my battery died.

Soon after I heard more deer coming down the same trail. When they got downwind, they turned inside out. I mean, they absolutely lost it, and they let every deer within hearing range know it. That, obviously, made me curious. So I used that unit the whole season and realized that it was working better than any other scent-control product I'd used. And it was dynamite for treating my clothes on trips. I still wasn't totally convinced, however.

To fully get there, I decided to see if I could trick my bird dog. I had a golden retriever at the time that I'd trained to find antlers, so I messed around with scent-eliminating sprays, Ozonics, and latex gloves. There was no comparison between the scent-eliminating sprays I tried (I didn't use them all, obviously) and the ozone treatment. It fooled my bird dog so much better than the sprays. It wasn't even close. That was convincing, because a good bird dog doesn't miss much with its nose. Kind of like a deer…

I do also use knee-high rubber boots whenever I can. I treat them with ozone as well, although you're not supposed to because eventually ozone will break down the adhesives used to hold them together. (This is also the reason you shouldn't use ozone in any way where you can continuously smell it, because that means it's also going directly into your lungs, which is not where you want a bleaching agent to be.)

Treated knee-highs can trick a dog to some extent as well, so I feel that a deer that crosses my trail won't realize how recently I've walked through. I can remember so many times when I was younger where a deer would cross my path after I'd walked in, and I knew that it was over for that particular deer. This was back when we used whatever leather boots we had and didn't have access to good scent-control options, of course. These days, I watch far more deer either cross my path and not even notice it or, at the very least, not pay it too much mind. That's a big win when it comes to being successful while bowhunting public land.

Of course, if you buy cheap rubber boots you'll hate them. You can pick up a $50 pair anywhere, but they'll probably only stay waterproof for a little while, if they ever actually were waterproof. They'll also be uncomfortable and ill-fitting. Good knee-highs are a must, not only for the day-to-day activities of scouting and hunting, but for those times when you suddenly need to drag a buck half a mile to your truck. You don't want to have a cheap pair of knee-highs on then, trust me.

Other Essentials: Coffee. Caffeine is my drug of choice these days, and there is nothing I love more than taking that first sip of coffee after I've sat for an hour or two, especially when it's cold outside. A traveling mug of coffee can keep me sitting an extra hour, and I've never seen a true downside from to freely off of a treestand, so there isn't much of a reason to not let fly when you need to. In a feeble attempt to consume less caffeine at one point in my life, I did take a Thermos of hot chocolate into the stand with me during a December sit. I thought I'd be able to reward myself with a sip every once in a while just like I did with coffee. That's not how my brain works, and when that delicious, toasty hot chocolate hit my lips, I was powerless not to chug it. So I did. And then I realized I don't have the self-control to bring hot chocolate into a stand and went back to coffee, which is very, very difficult to chug.

If I'm going to sit all day, I take plenty of food as well. Usually that consists of some sandwiches, fruit, and assorted candy. Again, if I'm not comfortable, I don't sit as long as I should, so I work hard to make things as cushy as I can. This also often includes a paperback book if I'm going to sit for more than about four hours.

I know a lot of hunters who scoff at that idea, but fortunately for me I don't care what they think. I enjoy reading, and I enjoy sitting in the woods. Sometimes I combine them, sometimes I don't. I much prefer reading on stand to surfing the internet or playing games on my phone. But that's just me. Do what you have to in order to ride out the long sits.

Get-Rich-Quick Products: Aside from scent-control questions, I get asked an awful lot about calling and decoying deer. My answers are usually pretty disappointing. I rarely call, and I very rarely decoy. I also rarely use scents. Having grown up in a heavily hunted state like Minnesota where our gun season is one of the earliest in the country, I'm just not that dependent on tricks.

I didn't grow up getting to bowhunt the rut, when most of those things are more effective, so they never became part of my arsenal. I do know plenty of Iowa and Kansas residents who take a different stance on the topic, but they also don't spend much time on public land, which leads to my main reason for going light on get-rich-quick products.

Every hunter I run into on public, which is a lot of hunters, has a grunt tube hanging around his neck. A lot of them also have a set of rattling antlers strapped to their backpacks, and judging by the amount of scent wicks I find hanging in random trees, they aren't shy about using olfactory attractants either. Everyone is looking for a shortcut, it seems, and they use them every chance they can. I'm only guessing here, but it sure seems to me like that would make the deer at least a little suspicious about any grunt they hear or whiff of sexy doe they get a snootful of.

That's not to say I haven't called in bucks on public land or decoyed them in, because I have. But it's not usually a part of my original plan. It usually stems from some experience that convinces me that the moment is right.

For example, a few years ago I spent time in a pine tree in Nebraska watching bucks chase does through a random patch of cedars but never down the ridge and past my stand like I expected. At that time, I didn't think I could move into the small island of trees, so I packed in a collapsible doe decoy. The first deer I saw was a good eight-pointer, and after a few bleats with my mouth, he turned in my direction and got close enough to rake some sumac and open himself up for a shot. It was the right situation, with the right deer.

I did also run into a buck in a chunk of big-woods public timber in Wisconsin one time that had already browsed past me before I knew he was there. Grunting had no effect on him, but when I snort-wheezed with my mouth his body language changed. It took four more snort-wheezes before he turned and came in, raking brush and posturing the whole time. It was pretty impressive behavior for mid-October, and I can safely say I was shaking pretty hard by the time I watched him tip over with my lighted nock buried in his offside shoulder.

That buck, while a really cool experience on public land, also solidified something I believe that most hunters don't. The snort-wheeze is not just a dominant buck call that works only during the rut. I've called in spikes in September and all sizes of bucks throughout the season. There is something to a snort-wheeze that will send certain bucks high-tailing it in the opposite direction, but not all of them. I don't know why, but it works really well on certain deer at certain times, and those deer don't need to be 6.5-year-olds and that time doesn't need to be November 11th. Trust me.

There is an important point to make when discussing ways to trick whitetails into range, no matter your strategy. Whitetails become much more susceptible to your chicanery if you are in the right spot, or really close to it. Making scents, calls, and decoys work on naturally skeptical deer is a matter of getting in where they really feel comfortable.

Think of it this way: when you turn on the Outdoor Channel you can watch a dozen big bucks each night sprint across picked cornfields to the rattling of the shows' hosts. That's probably not going to happen to you when you're sitting in a tree on public land in Pennsylvania.

If you've done your homework, you might have a buck sneak through 75 yards away, and while he's doing that, a couple of soft grunts or a tickling of the tines might bring him the extra 45 yards closer, because covering that distance in a place he feels secure is not a big risk. However, that same buck has heard hunters rattle dozens of times in his life and is simply not going to risk his neck to see what is going on three ridges away just because he hears some bone clack together. If you're in his bedroom, maybe he'll walk over if you reach out to him, but if he has to cover too much ground it's just not going to happen.

The main point of all this is that these things become crutches for us because they promise deer action. The problem is they don't deliver very often, even on private properties. On public, the odds of a deer reacting positively are even lower. Use them in the right situation, but make sure you understand how to get into the right situation first. You have to put in the requisite amount of work to find the right spots and then set up correctly to reap any real benefit out of these get-rich-quick products. This is just how it is, and it's best to think of them as a last step after you've set yourself up to succeed.

Now, all of this gear talk may make it may sound prohibitively expensive to outfit yourself properly to hunt public land, but it's not when you consider the cost of an average lease or buying a property outright. That's an obvious, but impossible to overstate, benefit of public land. We get to hunt it essentially for free. Remember that when you start looking at the price tags hanging off the best clothing on the market...

6

AMBUSH SITES OF ALL VARIETIES

One of the best things about hunting private ground is getting stand sites set up and prepped weeks or months before the season opens. The public land bowhunter often doesn't have that option, unfortunately. You can, however, get as close to set up as possible, which definitely alleviates some of the headaches.

For example, strewn across multiple states are specific trees on public land with which I'm very familiar. I've sat in some of them; others I just plan to sit at some point. All of them are marked on my maps, and all of them are suitable for an impromptu hunt.

I know this because I've put in the legwork in the off-season, or I've found them during the season while speed scouting. There's one particular tree I think about quite a bit that is located on a tract of Managed Forest Land in northern Wisconsin. It's a burr oak that grows on the edge of a swamp. The tree sits right on the lip of a six-foot drop-off, at the bottom of which immediately begins the wet stuff. It's located about as far from any easy access as possible, and it's smack dab in the middle of a seven-year-old clear cut.

On most of the property, you'll find poplar slash so thick that it's nearly impossible to set up in because you'd never be able to shoot. That oak tree, however, has a few towering oak tree buddies near it that have shaded out the undergrowth, creating a small island of open ground in the middle of all of the thick stuff. The swamp and the tiny ridge next to it serve to funnel deer movement, and due to the lay of the land, any wind out of the west or north is perfect for the tree.

The property on which it grows gets hunted hard, but not very well. The rifle hunters blaze away in there, but it's just too thick to kill off significant numbers of deer. That makes it an ideal spot for bucks to cruise, and they do. I know this because of the rubs I find during my scouting missions and grouse hunts on the property. Each January and February, some of the bucks that are responsible for making those rubs also drop an antler or two for my buddies and me to find. Almost every winter we find at least one big, Iowa-quality shed in addition to smaller, run-of-the-mill scrapper headgear.

The thing about the tree is that I've never hunted out of it. I've scouted the property obsessively, but I've always gotten distracted by other ground and other deer. Eventually, someday, I will hunt it though. And although it might not pan out to be an awesome setup, I don't believe that. I believe it'll be good, and the best part is, it's just waiting there for me to sneak in and hunt it.

If you have to, suss out the best trees ahead of time. I know this isn't always possible, especially if you have to travel quite a way to get to your spot. Every year I hunt new out-of-state public parcels, and other than what I've seen on aerial photography, I show up blind.

This requires a different eye toward stand sites, but you should always start with the digital scouting clues. Occasionally you can find specific trees to set up in and kill deer, but it's rare. I've done it a couple of times. The first time was in Oklahoma where I could see a lone tree on the edge of a state-planted oat field. I set up in that tree and nearly killed a great buck before arrowing a doe later in the evening.

The other time was during my first South Dakota public land whitetail hunt. My original spots had failed me (or I failed at hunting them correctly), so I looked at my Plan B pond and picked out a patch of oak trees that looked promising. When I hiked in with a stand, they were smaller than I imagined but big enough, and leafed-out enough, to work. Four hours into my first sit I had a young doe trot through, followed by two grunting bucks. The first buck, a young six-pointer, sprinted by me at a distance of maybe 10 feet.

The second buck, a deer that had blue baling twine wrapped all over his nontypical antlers, wasn't so lucky. Although not my largest buck, that crazy-looking deer is by far one of my favorites. And he died because of a tree I found through aerial photography, long before setting out on the hunt.

This strategy is much easier on more open ground where hotspot trees are far more evident. When you're dealing with more timber, it's a matter of getting in and seeing where you should sit. This is somewhat of a lost art.

It used to be that we'd go out and walk through the woods until we saw sign, and then we'd set up and hunt the deer where they wanted to be. Now we do everything in our power to reverse that plan and make the deer come to us. From bait to food plots to calls, decoys, scents, and lures, we work pretty hard to contrive situations where the deer will be conditioned or prompted to travel to where we want to hunt, not necessarily where they naturally want to be. On public land, that's either simply not an option or not a very good idea.

You've got to learn to go where the deer want to be, and that involves carrying your lightweight setup and looking for sign, terrain features, and general deer-friendly stuff until you find your spot. Then you need to find a tree.

This is the other reason I like to use small stands, because I often end up in small or crooked trees. I'm a big believer of making a spot work in any way I can. That often means setting up in dinky trees that sway with every movement I make. Some hunters won't set up in small-diameter trees believing that they'll get busted by sharp-eyed deer, and to some extent, they are right.

That's a risk I'll take every time, however, because I find when I hunt where deer don't expect to encounter humans, they don't look up quite as much. I still get busted every year, usually by does who seem to have nothing better to do than stare, stomp, and snort, but again, that's a risk I'll take. It seems like bucks are less likely to bust you in that situation, because as much as we believe they are super cagey and nearly unkillable, I don't buy that. They walk through the woods like they own the place, and if anyone in the deer herd is on their A-game for spotting hunters, it's often the does and not the bucks.

Naturally, you don't have to go airborne to kill bucks. Ground blinds are all the rage these days. Unfortunately, using pop-ups on public ground isn't much fun. It's really not much fun if you're not allowed to trim brush, because if you can't brush in a hub-style blind, you're not going to kill too many deer out of it.

If you can brush a blind in, you've got a chance. In other situations you can cram a blind in-between some cedar trees and allow nature to sort of envelop it. Or you might just stumble upon something manmade that allows you to shove a blind next to it and fool passing bucks.

I ran into a situation like that on a recent hunt in South Dakota on a Walk-

In ranch in the middle of the state. To be honest, it was a trio of decent mule deer bucks that brought my attention to a weird little spot that was conducive to setting up a ground blind.

The area where I saw the bucks consisted of a single ridge that had been cleared off during the last few years. Ground-hugging cedars once shaded out the undergrowth along its length, but it's now clear of all trees where the rancher went in and cut them out of about a five-acre area. I don't know why, honestly, but can hypothesize it might have been to encourage fresh growth for the cattle.

For some reason, every time we drove by that spot we'd see whitetails or mule deer in there, so one day in the pouring rain I carried a blind in. I knew that the scrub cedars and junipers ringing the ridgetop would never accommodate a stand, so my only option was to dig into the turkey hunter's playbook. There was a convenient pile of cedar skeletons from the land-clearing job, so I pushed my blind up next to it and just sort of backed it into the pile. It wasn't a great setup, but it looked better than I expected it to.

Two mornings later, I crawled into the blind during a light drizzle with plenty of time to spare before I'd be able to see my pins. Twenty minutes into shooting light, a goofball buck stepped into my only shooting lane and started to groom himself. After hunting in the pouring rain for a few days I gave him a hard look and even clipped my release on—twice.

The problem was that the buck looked like the Grinch's dog when he puts branches on his head to mimic a reindeer right before they ride into town to ruin Christmas in Whoville. I hemmed and hawed for a long time on whether to shoot the buck anyway, but better judgment finally won out. Almost as soon as it did, I watched a wide, tall rack pop out of the brush closer to my blind. The second deer was a no-question 10-pointer that ended up scoring exactly 145 inches. All of that was made possible by a ground blind.

Now, even with such a positive experience under my belt, I'm still not a huge fan of hub-style blinds for deer hunting. When it comes to ground blinds on public land, I often go *au naturel*. I used to hunt out of natural blinds a lot when I was a youngster, and although I never set the world on fire kill-wise, I did have some encounters that left an indelible impression.

At some point, I got away from them, but I've come full circle. The first big buck I killed on public land was crossing a river and walking between some cottonwoods that were so large around it was impossible to hang a stand in them. I had no choice but to set up behind one of the cottonwoods like I was playing hide and seek. The buck crossed the river and walked toward me, never once paying attention to the camo-clad hunter peeking out from behind the gray trunk of a cottonwood I'm positive he'd walked by hundreds of times in his life. He passed by at 20 yards, and he didn't even look my way when I drew. Since then, I've killed a few more that way. I use natural blinds a lot when treestands just aren't an option or if the wind just doesn't allow me to hunt a spot the way I want to.

The thing about natural blinds is that you've got to consider the cover on all sides of you, but especially behind you. Everyone knows that you need some cover in front, but ignoring your backdrop is a bad idea. I tend to pick a natural deadfall or good-sized tree to use as my base and then use dead branches and anything else I can to build a natural-looking blind.

I always kick the leaves out until I'm down to bare ground as well. If you're worried about the noise, do this the way turkeys scratch, which is a pattern of scratch-scratch, pause, and then scratch. This is no joke. Once in a while you even call in a turkey if you do it right, which isn't a desirable outcome because then they bust you and putt-putt their way out of sight—or, worse, fly off.

No matter what woodland critter you mimic to get the job done, just make sure you do it. I like to kneel a lot when I'm in a natural blind, and if I have to shift my weight slightly from discomfort or to try to get into shooting position, I don't want to lean awkwardly on a stick or some leaves and draw attention to myself. Make sure you're settled on bare dirt so that you have a fighting chance of not getting busted by close-proximity deer, which have a very low tolerance for humans sitting on the ground near them.

If you are going to sit in natural blinds, you'll probably want to leave your smartphone in your pocket and skip any light reading to pay full attention. It's very possible for a deer to sneak up on a hunter in a treestand, but in a ground blind it's different. When they are within range and you're at their level, they'll bust you as you're making the slightest movement. Usually that movement involves peeking around the tree after you realize there is a deer in your lap. Don't let that happen.

Occasionally, they completely ignore natural ground blinds and feed right up to you. I had a young buck do this to me on public land in Minnesota one evening, and while I wanted to arrow one of the does with him, I couldn't move. He ended up feeding so close that I could hear his jaw working as he chewed right next to me. He was one of the few wild deer I've had that I could have touched. In fact, for about 30 seconds I could have probably picked his nose and wiped a booger on his antler. It was awesome.

Another time, more recently, I had to bail out of my stand in North Dakota because the wind was blowing so hard that we were under an actual High Wind Advisory. If you've ever been to North Dakota, you know they don't take run-of-the-mill gusts as anything too serious, so for them to issue an advisory you have to be on the verge of being a human tumbleweed at any moment. Why I even tried to sit in that stand in 50-plus-mph winds is anyone's guess, and while I won't claim it was my most intelligent moment, I blame a gnarly old 10-pointer that was awfully reliable in his river-crossing habits. Even knowing that buck was coming couldn't keep me in that cottonwood, however.

I climbed down and made a hasty blind in a fallen trunk of a much larger cottonwood, and as the light faded, seven does and a young buck fed in. The lead doe was so close I could have tossed an arrow and hit her. When the buck made it to 20 yards, I thumped him. Not a minute later, the 10-pointer waded across the river and walked right by my stand. It was a bittersweet moment for sure, but it was further proof that the right natural ground blind can be truly deadly.

For this type of hunting, I use a good cushion but rarely use a chair or stool. It's not that comfortable to only use a cushion, but I find that I have much better encounters if I'm sitting on my knees versus sitting on a stool or a chair. If you have the right setup, you can get away with it, but in my experience finding that setup isn't all that easy.

No matter what you do when it comes to your ambush sites, how you go about them will affect your entire hunt far more than any other decision you make. So do all of the homework you can, do the most pre-season work you can, and choose wisely.

And for the love of God, plan your entrance and exit routes.

This means something more than just marking a trail so you don't get turned around when you head into the woods, although you might need that too. A good route does allows you to get in and out quietly, without getting spotted or smelled. This is easier said than done, which is why I think a lot of bowhunters don't pay as much attention to this step.

The deer that you're going to encounter on stand are always on your mind, but what about the deer that are bedded in the patch of gray dogwood halfway to your hotspot? You blow them out, and they might take the whole woods with them. You might not even know that you blew them out, which I guess is probably easier to stomach than watching a couple of stark-white tails disappear into the underbrush and then hear the snorting of a whole doe group.

Now, it's not possible to *not* spook deer every time you go into and out of the woods. But it is possible to think about how you'll get there and back, and for some ambush sites, a little extra work can go a long way toward having more action night after night, or morning after morning.

Not only do you need to plan your routes in according to the deer you might bump into or get winded by, but you've got to plan your way out. I've already mentioned my affinity for flowing water and its tendency to allow me to get to deer without spooking them, but it's not just rivers and streams that you can use.

Gullies, ditches, general low spots, and even the back sides of ridges can get you where you need to be. Take a long look at the terrain and try to figure out a way to get to your spot that causes the least amount of ripples in the deer woods. It's almost always necessary to go farther than you'd like, but that's what public land hunting is all about. If it were easy, the hunting celebs would do it, right?

There are times when you just can't get to a hotspot all that quietly, like, say, mid-to-late October when the forest floor is covered in leaves that aren't unlike walking through acres of potato chips. In this situation, what do you do?

Sometimes you've just got to walk through them and cross your fingers. This is another situation where sometimes I'll try to sound like turkeys. At least to my knowledge, there has never been too much predation on deer by longbeards, so whitetails are pretty accepting of turkeys in their neighborhood. Not only do I try to walk like a turkey, I usually carry a mouth call in my pocket and will softly yelp my way through.

This can work, although it's not foolproof because you are, after all, calling attention to yourself. This is bad enough when there is a buck bedded close by, but worse when someone is fall turkey hunting with an either-sex tag and might want to send a load of 5s in your general direction. Be careful if you're going to try this trick.

The main point is to try, try as hard as you can, to spook as few deer as possible when you go in to hunt. This seems obvious enough, but it should start the moment you park and extend to the moment you get back to the truck. For many hunters, it really doesn't, and that's one of the reasons why most bowhunters won't fill a single tag the entire season.

In fact, when you're thinking about where to park in relation to your stand, consider doing exactly the opposite of what you'd expect most hunters to do. Park as far away from your stand as you can. As long as you don't have to park in a specific spot or parking lot for the land you're hunting, it's always a good idea to park the truck quite a way from where you plan to hunt and then walk in. This is the exact opposite strategy of most hunters I meet. They would gladly drive their trucks or ATVs right up to theirs stand if they could. When you're planning your stand and blind sites, think about that. Think about how you can work harder to keep the deer in the dark about your presence, because it can make all of the difference in the world.

7

CONTROL WHAT YOU CAN CONTROL

At any given point, during any given hunt, there will be many things that you just can't control. Other hunters walking by—or through—your spot are a given. I don't know how many times I've watched hunters walk by me while I was hunting, but it has happened a lot.

It has happened with small game hunters. Upland hunters. Duck hunters. I've had hikers go by, and horseback riders as well. I've had ranchers drive through rounding up cattle, and I've had people fish right past my river-crossing stands. I had a kid walk past me one time shouting, "Who let the dogs out!" over and over again.

And of course, I've had loads of bowhunters walk into my setup. One particularly memorable encounter occurred when I was sitting on some public dirt in South Dakota, in the rain, on the edge of a cut cornfield. The field was littered with tracks, and it was one of those nights where deer like to move early, so I was hyper alert.

When I heard the first tickling of tines I couldn't quite pin it down. As the bucks really started to get after it, I clipped on and got ready because it sounded like they were going to fight their way right past me. After maybe half a minute the sound didn't quite jive with a buck fight, and I realized, moments before they walked through, that it sounded more like plastic hitting trees.

The first hunter nearly stepped on me as he lugged a full-body decoy through the cedars, but he didn't see me. Neither did his buddy. I listened to that hard plastic decoy scrape and bang its way into the area I was sure the deer were using to bed. I never saw a deer that night, and that was largely out of my control.

You'll deal with other humans on public land. That's just part of the deal. So is unpredictable weather. Even though you'd really like it to dawn cold, crisp, and just right for deer movement, there is nothing that says it will. Or at least not when you've got a free morning to climb 17 feet up a tree.

It's far better to pay attention to the things you actually can control and then do your best to actually control them. For example, are you a good shot with your bow? I mean, can you actually make a shot when it counts, not just hit a paper plate at 25 yards?

That matters. Being a good shot boils down to confidence, and you can control how confident you are in your shooting. Naturally, this starts with decent gear that is set up specifically for you. I don't know how many people I see at the range every year who are shooting hand-me-down bows that don't fit them at all.

If you don't care about being a good shot, a hand-me-down is the way to go. Now, I'm not saying you shouldn't take a free bow if it comes your way. Not everyone has money for a new one. I get that. But if you take a bow that is set up for someone else, it won't shoot very well for you. Long before you need to worry about being a good shot, you need to worry about being set up exactly how you need to be. That is 100 percent within your control.

After that, if you can shoot well and you engage in enough practice, you'll be able to shoot well where it matters most: in the woods. Although anyone with a few seasons under his or her belt knows that being able to shoot well at home doesn't always mean much in the woods.

The best way to bridge that gap is to practice like you mean it. Get a 3D target and set it up for different angles and different shooting scenarios. Learn where your point of impact should be on all angles, and make it second nature to put your appropriate pin where it needs to be.

Control how well you can shoot, because if we're being honest here, there might only be one shot opportunity that comes your way this season. Maybe less, maybe more, but it's not likely that any public land bowhunter is going to get a whole bunch of mulligans until he finally settles the right pin behind a buck's shoulder and makes good on an opportunity. Make your shots count by preparing for them ahead of time through quality practice that is designed to make you a better bowhunter.

And please, please, please practice with broadheads. Or, at the very least, match your arrows to actual broadheads that you have shot. The bowhunting industry has done well for itself by selling broadheads that promise to fly like your field points. In my experience, this sometimes happens, sometimes doesn't. It often varies from arrow to arrow and broadhead to broadhead, even out of the same package.

It doesn't matter whether you're a die-hard fixed-blade fan or a mechanical shooter, when you screw in a broadhead after practicing all summer with field points, there is a solid chance that your point of impact will change with that arrow. You do not want to figure that out on a deer halfway through the season, so invest some time into shooting with actual broadheads. That allows you to fill your quiver with arrows that will go where you point them when you're actually hunting. I can't stress this enough.

Another thing you can control is how in shape you are. Hunting athletes are all the rage these days, but even so, that mentality isn't overly strong in the whitetail crowd. This is probably because with the right ground, you can kill a buck without burning a calorie.

In the real world, where you actually have to hunt, that's not the case, so you'll need to consider how physically capable you are. Generally, the better shape you're in, the better you'll hunt. I used to think that wasn't true, because I didn't want it to be so, but now I believe it fully.

I'm in the best shape of my life as I write this, and it has to do with a commitment to being healthier overall. I started running and lifting weights several years ago, largely because I wanted to be a good father to my then one-year-old twin daughters. While those little girls are much older, they are still a driving force in my life that keeps me focused on being in shape.

A most-welcome side benefit I realized after starting to become more physically fit was that I started to enjoy scouting more, and I didn't dread hanging stands nearly as much. In fact, the whole process of hunting became more enjoyable, including just sitting on a stand with a lower back that wouldn't start barking after an hour or two.

You can control how in shape you are, and while most people won't work out solely to be a better hunter, it's a good idea regardless of your motivations. The fact that you will undoubtedly work harder at all facets of hunting is a very nice bonus if nothing else.

Remember that while there are plenty of frustrating things that are simply cosmic whims totally beyond your control, there are things that are within your grasp. Control them and mold them into advantages for you in the field.

They'll help you in ways you can't imagine.

8

EARLY SEASON AND THE RULE OF OPPOSITES

Opening day is like Christmas morning for bowhunters. For me it's a ritual, just like it is for most of us. The only opening day I've ever missed in Minnesota was due to a wedding, and believe me when I say this, I tried pretty hard to get out of it.

I failed, mostly because my wife got the final say.

For the public land bowhunter, opening day is a blessing and a curse. If you live in a state like I do where small game season opens the same day as archery, then you're going to deal with squirrel and bunny hunters as well as your fellow whitetail addicts.

I can remember, not so fondly, sitting in a treestand on opening morning of the 2012 season in a backup spot on a property in the Twin Cities. My first choice, a place I'd scouted religiously, was occupied by a guy with severe boundary issues and the hunting ethics of a weasel.

I'd gone in the night before the season to lay out my sticks and stand at the base of my chosen tree. The spot consisted of a peninsula of woods jutting into a cattail slough where the deer liked to cross. An eight-pointer that was all of 135 inches would cross the spot every couple of mornings in a not-too-consistent manner. But it was consistent enough to hinge my opening morning hopes on.

The problem was that while I was quietly laying out the makings of my setup, another hunter walked in on me. He waved and laid a stand of his own on the ground, and then he walked up to me and asked if I was planning to hunt there.

I don't know if he thought I carried a treestand into the woods for some reason other than hunting, but I told him that, yes, I was planning on sneaking in early and sitting the stand in the morning. He then put his hands on his hips, looked around, and said, "Well, I'll just set up over there then."

He pointed to a tree not 50 yards away. When I told him we wouldn't do each other much good sitting basically right next to one another, he told me that he'd shoot them if they came from one way and I could shoot them if they came from the other. Because I knew I was already hosed, I said, "Well, that might work. But I can shoot at least 80 yards so I could probably get them before they get to you."

He didn't know what to say and looked awfully relieved when I loaded up my stand and left. I don't want to make eye contact with some stranger when I'm bowhunting deer. I just don't. So I hiked to my backup spot. I knew that the small game hunters would be thick in the woods in the morning and figured that some deer would get pushed past my new stand, which was located on a power line at the far end of the public parcel. It was situated as a natural funnel without the added pressure of a bunch of rimfire-rifle-toting hunters, so I thought it was possible that I'd have a few four-legged escapees walk past.

The following morning I parked my truck and hiked in early. Really early. At first light things were pretty quiet, but it didn't take long before the .22s were popping off in the distance and a four-pointer streaked past my stand. He was the only deer I saw that morning, because I got wigged out by the .22 bullets I heard going past me. I don't know about anyone else, but I lose a lot of my desire to sit in a tree when I can hear that curious "zzzzzz" sound of a bullet going past. It's happened a few times and never made me feel super good about what I had going on at the moment.

I'm positive I'm not the only bowhunter to experience something like that on opening weekend. It happens. A lot of times the woods are an absolute circus during those first few days. In that capacity, I feel almost like a rifle hunter sitting there with his fingers crossed, hoping a buck gets pushed past and not thinking at all about natural deer movement. That's my least favorite kind of hunting.

But I go, and you probably do as well, if for no other reason than to shake the cobwebs of the off-season away and get back into the bowhunting groove. Of course, if I'm hunting a random spot in a low-pressure state, I feel a lot better about hunting opening weekend. Not too long ago I was considering which of my stands I'd hunt during South Dakota's opening day when I kept getting bad news wind-wise. The only good stand I had for the wind was occupied by a buddy of mine, which meant it was time to call an audible.

There was a too-easy-to-be-good pond on a Walk-In ranch I'd found that I wanted to hunt, but it was 200 yards from the parking area and, I figured, a sure thing for hunting pressure. With nothing to lose, I drove past the property anyway and couldn't believe there wasn't a single vehicle parked there. Not one.

It took me about three minutes to go from the truck to the tree in which I wanted to set up, and as an added vote of confidence I jumped a buck bedded directly beneath it. I strapped on my sticks in the afternoon heat and sweated my way up to about 17 feet. I'd just snapped on my safety harness when I heard something coming. A buck, on a dead run, crested the ridge directly behind me and stopped at 15 yards.

He was good enough to shoot, but the problem was that my bow was on the ground. The buck stopped and stared at the pond, thinking, I can only imagine, thirsty thoughts. Every 10 seconds he'd shake his head to clear it of flies. Every time he did, I'd move. First I retrieved my release and put it on, then I kneeled down and took hold of my rope. Slowly, I lifted my bow as he shook away pests.

I'd hung my stand facing away from where I expected the deer to come, which gave me a chance. When I got my bow in my hand I untied my rope and nocked an arrow. By then he was slurping pond water and in an excellent position to shoot. It was one the shortest hunts I've ever had for any buck, anywhere.

Those encounters are far less common than we'd like. Most of the time, it doesn't work out that way. That's one of the reasons why I like it when the first week of the season has come and gone and the fervor of opening weekend dies down. That's when the deer seem to settle down and move more, and that's when you should hunt more, but maybe not when you think you should be out there. My early-season style is contrarian, but it works. And it's all about opposites.

Hunt The Heat: No one likes hunting when it's 90 degrees out. I get that. It's uncomfortable, and if you were to believe everything we are told about whitetails, you're wasting your time hunting then because the deer won't move. I had one old-timer, a guy who was considered a whitetail expert, tell me it was a biological fact that bucks couldn't move when the temperature got to a certain point. I guess he was probably right, but the temperature would have probably had to hit about 300 degrees for it to be true.

Deer move in the heat, but that movement depends on a few things. First off, if you're hunting the early part of the season they are simply more accustomed to the warmer temperatures. In 2013 I found a bachelor group of six bucks in North Dakota that contained a great 10-pointer in full velvet when the season opened. I set a stand on a crossing for him and waited for midafternoon to roll around before going in. When I got out of my truck, it was 91 degrees and the wind was blowing up to 35 miles per hour. When I opened my driver's side door and stepped onto the cracked dirt of the two-track, it was like stepping out into an oven.

The tree I wanted to sit was almost exactly one mile from where you can park, so suffice it to say I was a sweaty mess by the time I climbed into my stand, which unfortunately was facing dead west. It was an indescribable relief when the sun finally dipped behind some of the jagged peaks that are the hallmark of the Badlands.

And as soon as it did, the deer started to move in spite of the heat. It was still hot, and ungodly windy, but I saw four bucks pass by out of range. Then I saw the big boy with his nose dipped into the river and his velvet antlers poking out of the brush. He crossed right to me, just like he was supposed to, and I missed him.

I just plain missed him. At 20 yards, no less.

It was so windy he didn't even know that I'd shot, and he didn't notice when I nocked another arrow. He was, at the time, the biggest buck I'd gotten a crack at on public land, and I forced myself to aim with all my might on the second shot. It must have worked because he died on the far bank of that river. Conventional wisdom would suggest that no deer should have been moving that night, but they were, just as they had when the temperatures were 20 degrees cooler.

I've seen that happen on public land enough to believe that it's worth hunting unseasonably hot weather every chance you can. In fact, I look forward to the hot weather now because I know that I can usually sit over water and see deer, and I'm not nearly as likely to run into other hunters. Pressure is the enemy. Remember that—always.

Of course, killing a buck when the thermometer is topped out isn't as simple as just going hunting. You've got to have an early-season plan in place for taking advantage of the toasty conditions, and that should involve not only water, but also south winds.

Every year I think about my stand sites from a west or northwest wind direction, and every early season I'm hit with straight south winds that almost always usher in warm temperatures. These days, I try to plan to have a few spots where bucks can not only slake their thirst or maybe get a belly full of greenery, but also that I can hunt when the wind blows from the Equator on up. Plan for both, and you can kill deer—like that big velvet public land buck that gave me a redemption shot—when most bowhunters think it's a waste of time to be on stand at all.

Gusty Stuff: That 151-inch North Dakota buck was on his feet and active well before dark during oppressive heat and some of the windiest conditions I've ever hunted. High wind, like sauna-level heat, isn't much fun to hunt in, but the deer will still move. A lot of people say they won't, but that's just silly. If deer didn't move in windy conditions, there'd be bucks that starved to death in their beds in Kansas and a few other tree-deprived middle-America states where the windmills never stop spinning.

Whitetails are going to eat and drink water every day, regardless of the conditions. If it's the rut, they are going to seek out amenable ladies. They live in the wild and deal with wind and heat all the time. They've got stuff figured out much better than we do, and so what we perceive to affect their behavior either really doesn't or doesn't to the degree we often believe.

Of all the miserable conditions in which to hunt, wind is my least favorite, but it's worked in my favor enough to keep me out there when I should be flying kites or sailing. A few years ago I was working on some bucks on public land in Minnesota when October rolled around and the mercury rose. With it, a strong south wind moved in, and I had a hard time convincing myself to hunt. I did, but mostly to observe a specific spot, so I parked myself in a natural blind and picked up my binoculars.

I saw an old friend from the summer come out and feed, and then a smaller buck and a few does. The wind was absolutely smoking, but the deer didn't seem to care, and I firmly believe it's because the conditions had kept most of the hunters away. In fact, I think it kept them all away except for me, because the parking lot was empty and that's not something I ever expect to see in that spot during any evening in October.

As I watched, a nine-pointer made a scrape beneath an oak tree. Occasionally he'd rake his antlers in the overhanging limbs, and soon enough a young eight-pointer wandered over. As if they planned it, both bucks started making scrapes next to one another. The dirt in my neck of the woods is extremely sandy, so when it's dry it gets really dusty. For maybe two or three minutes those two bucks had clouds of dust rising off their hooves like exhaust, and then they went their separate ways.

I'm not big into scrape hunting, but I'm not a total fool either, and if the big guy in the sky was giving this lowly deer hunter a sign to sit over scrapes, I believe that might have been it. The following night I sneaked in and hung a stand over the dished-out scrape the larger buck had created. The wind was still whipping across the landscape, yet the first deer I saw that night was the nine-pointer.

I could hardly believe it as he emerged from a cattail swamp, an hour and a half before dark. I knew the deer from summer scouting, but until the previous night hadn't laid eyes on him for months. But there he was, sauntering through the wind-bent cattails and into the rye field over which I was perched.

He hovered around in rifle range, but he didn't get any closer and there was nothing I could do to entice him in my direction. He would have never heard me call over the wind, so I settled in and decided to see how things would unfold.

What unfolded was that he fed out of sight and a doe started working in from the opposite direction. As she neared me I figured it was about time to fill my freezer. Then I caught movement out of the corner of my eye. The buck was at about 10 yards and rubbing his antlers on a cedar. When he stepped into his scrape, I shot him. I remember a lot of things about that hunt, but what was most vivid was the way the wind whipped away the dirt and dust uncoiling from underneath his pounding hooves as he bolted across the field.

Well, that, and the fact that he died in the middle of a pond so I had to wade out into chest-deep water to get a hold of his antlers. But mostly, I remember how frickin' windy it was and how he didn't seem to mind moving in those gusty conditions at all.

A Bit Of Precipitation: If I had to pick my favorite miserable condition in which to hunt, it wouldn't take me long to deliberate. Rain is my favorite. By far. In fact, I don't consider it miserable at all. I love hunting in the rain.

I absolutely love it.

Anything from a drizzle to a steady rain is perfect. Give me a decent rain any day, and I'll sit on stand or in a ground blind. Most hunters won't, which is perfect because I want the woods to myself. For some reason, the deer just seem to move in the rain. They do this all year, but they seem particularly prone to moving in the precipitation during the first half of the season.

It's important to note that you should hunt in the rain, but not in a thunderstorm. Lightning and treestands are a bad combination, so don't mix them. Rain, good old rain, is another matter altogether. If you want the woods to yourself and like to see deer movement, hunt then.

You'll probably be tempted to wear rain gear, I know sometimes I am. The problem with that is that rain gear is usually noisy, is oftentimes a bit too shiny, and tends to only slow down your soaking. I just wear whatever camo I want to and accept the fact that I'll be wet shortly after I get out there. If it's predicted to get cold, I'll use some level of rain gear, but otherwise, nope.

No matter your camo choice, if you're not into sitting on stand during a frog-choker and getting soaked, consider a still-hunt. I've only killed a few deer still-hunting in my life, but some of the best times I've spent in the woods have involved creeping along, molasses-slow, while looking for a deer.

This is easiest in the rain, when the deer should be on their feet and you can move quietly. Oftentimes, I use a morning or afternoon rain shower to still-hunt through an area I wanted to check out anyway. I figure that I'm far less likely to leave scent all over the place and can combine some scouting with a little hunting, so it's the best of both worlds. Because of the ability to move without making (much) sound, you can move a little faster than you can on dry days.

This may be more contrarian than most can handle, but hear me out. The greatest hunters of all times have all, at one point or another, given advice on still-hunting. All of it involves slowing down to the point where you're just barely moving. Some say that in the span of a couple of hours you should only cover 200 yards. Puke. If I wanted to stay in one spot while I was hunting, I would, I don't know, get into a gosh darn treestand.

I don't want to, though. I want to see the woods and run across a deer. The best way to do that is to cover some ground. Now, I'm not advocating sprinting through the woods and hoping to see a deer before it sees you, because that won't work. But you can slip along in a rainstorm slowly, but not so slowly that birds nest in your beard and moss grows on your nether region (you better hope that's moss!). Move slowly, but keep going. Use the rain as cover and pay attention to the wind.

Wednesdays Are Best: Most of us are yoked by adult responsibility, which means we can't hunt any time we want. That's unfortunate, especially if you don't have the chance to bowhunt public land midweek. Weekends, as we all know, are the most popular time for every waterhead in the county to decide it's time to spot-and-stalk Booners on public land, and that means the hunting is a lot more difficult on Saturday and Sunday.

The deer know this, and they react accordingly. By Wednesday, however, they seem to forget and start to move more. I love Wednesdays and Thursdays when I'm hunting heavily hunted public land for this reason, particularly in the early part of the season when it's far less likely that a whole bunch of hunters will take the week off to sit every day. If you have the chance, plan your hunts around lower hunter activity even if the difference is only a couple of days.

This, naturally, can be a season-long strategy as well. There is an inverse relationship to the ebb and flow of hunter hours in the woods and the amount of hours deer will be on the move during shooting light. The fewer hunters there are, the more deer are going to move. Hunting on a Wednesday instead of a Saturday isn't going to solve all of your problems, but it's a good start.

I had this point driven home to me in 2010 when I was getting my butt kicked by deer on public land in the Twin Cities. I was down to the wire time-wise and had yet to fill my tag. The weekend before gun opener had come and gone, along with the usual crowd trampling through the woods looking for the best spot to sit on opening morning.

It was a Tuesday night when I went for broke on a field edge where the deer tracks showed some serious traffic. I saw some does and a great buck cruise across the field in a very specific spot. There was a tiny rise in the field next to a drainage ditch that he seemed to follow. When I went to look at it closer, I saw that the deer were using the rise to cross from a point of woods to a ravine that led to a crossing on the Rum River.

I hung a stand there, and the following morning I walked out in the dark to sit. The stand I intended to hunt was tucked into a staging area, but the wind was all wrong. I panicked and, as the first real light of the day was settling in, glassed the field. A doe was standing right by my stand. Then she dropped down the hill toward the Rum River.

With nothing to lose, I sprinted through the drainage and popped up into the field. I ran to the stand, clipped on, and climbed up. I hadn't even pulled my face mask on when I saw him coming along, obviously following the doe's trail. He never made it out of the field. He turned out to be a six-pointer that scored just a smidge over 125 inches, making it one of my coolest bucks ever and an absolute gift on public land. I can't help but think a little part of the success on that hunt, besides dumb luck, was that it was Wednesday morning, and the crowd just wasn't there to spook the deer into the cover like they had been the previous weekend, or surely would be in a couple of days.

Do your best to forget what we are told about when deer move and when they don't. That hackneyed advice doesn't cut it for the public land bowhunter. Remember, most of the tips and tactics you're given about deer hunting come from hunters who never, ever set foot on public land. Knowing that, ask yourself how much value there can possibly be in their advice.

9

OCTOBER LOVE AND THE LIES OF THE LULL

To me, the October lull is the most glaring example of bowhunters secretly loving excuses not to hunt. As I've mentioned, I'm a Minnesotan, which means I don't count on the rut for my bowhunting success. Skipping half of October is not an option when I might only get a couple of days of November to hunt before the Orange Army takes over.

That means I've never given much credence to the lull, because it doesn't change my strategy at all. I do think an awful lot of bowhunters see diminished activity by about mid-October, but that's due to several reasons. Food sources are changing, of course. But I also believe it's largely due to pressure. I know that plenty of folks will disagree with that by saying they have prime ground under strict control and the buck movement still slows noticeably.

The reason for this is, in my opinion, is at least partially due to where we like to hunt and how we tend to look for deer. Bowhunters like being in places where they can see, which means field edges and stand sites that provide wide-open views. Those also happen to be some of the best places to hunt earlier in the season, and they're also the easiest stands to hunt.

The problem is that we tend to burn them out, and that means we see fewer deer. This coincides with early to mid-October, and then all of a sudden those same spots can turn on again in November. The prevailing thought is that the bucks moved early in the season, stopped moving in the middle, and started moving again as the rut approached.

I don't believe that to be true.

I know they move during what is supposed to be the dead part of the season, because I see them do it all the time. But my encounters almost always occur in the thick stuff, and they often correlate to mast or some other changing food source. So if you think deer aren't killable in October, think again.

Deer will make mistakes because they still have to drink. They still have to eat. If a cold front moves in, they'll make some scrapes and knock their antlers against their buddy's rack. I've found that this is true on private, but can be even more reliable on public land.

Where I hunt in Wisconsin, baiting is legal. This means that nearly all of the bowhunters and rifle hunters sit over a pile of corn or apples. Bait piles are everywhere during opening week, and again as the rifle season closes in and the rut is ramping up. Right in-between those two times, however, there seems to be a respite from the baiting and a nice little surge of deer movement.

To be honest, the first couple of weeks of October are the only time I can get on good, natural movement without feeling like every deer in the woods is filling their belly at a nearby bait pile a few minutes after dark. Now, I'm not ranting against baiting in general. I'm just explaining how I hunt around a bunch of hunters who do rely on piles of corn.

I've seen really good lull movement on public land where baiting wasn't allowed either, so that's not the sole source of the better action. It's all about the pressure, and when a good percentage of the hunting population stays home to watch football because they believe the deer hunting won't be any good, those public land deer will move. If you want to kill them, you should probably head out and sit.

It's not enough to focus your hunting time when others will likely stay home, however. That's just part of the strategy. The other part is to figure out where the deer like to be *right now*. This is easier said than done, and trail cameras can't do all the sleuthing for you. You need to think about why your stands aren't producing and then react.

Most of the time, as I've mentioned, they go cold because we sit them too much. That's usually only a component of it, though, and there tends to be more to the lack of activity than just stand-site burnout. Changing food sources are often the major influencer of October deer movement.

This is the time of year when agricultural harvest really kicks in throughout much of the best whitetail areas. Most of the standing soybeans will be gone as long as it wasn't overly wet in your area. Much of the standing corn will end up being combined as well, which changes things a lot.

Deer use standing corn for security cover, safe travel, and, of course, food. When 100 acres of it suddenly disappears in a 48-hour period, it's obviously going to change their patterns drastically.

Not only are many of their traditional destination food sources changing, but random deer buffets will be opening up or shutting down in the beginning of October as well. The most obvious example is hard mast, like acorns. A good acorn drop can influence deer to feed and travel in ways that they didn't in September. Any time a whitetail can fill its belly with a quality food source while staying in the cover, it will, and that is what acorns are all about.

Soft mast matters, too. In some of the states I hunt, apple trees are pretty common. The consistency with which they drop, and which ones are deer magnets, is anything but reliable, however. For example, some of the spots I hunt in southern Minnesota are dotted with wild apple trees that will drop hundreds of pounds of apples at a time. Oftentimes, I find rotting apples beneath the trees without any real evidence that the deer are eating the fruit at all.

In northern Wisconsin where I spend a fair amount of time, an individual apple tree that is loaded up can be the best place to hunt in an entire section. I know it probably has something to do with the availability of food in different regions, but I also know that I've watched those northern Wisconsin bucks walk right through and past a lot of different quality food sources to get to apples. And an apple tree in the thick stuff that is dropping during the beginning of October is like a winning lottery ticket.

Setting The Stage: The thing about hunting early October is that you might figure out a changing food source situation as it's happening and kill a buck. You also might just have to rely on staging areas off of the destination food sources deer use all season. This is my single best strategy for killing mature bucks, and it's crucial for public land success.

Naturally, you've got to know what a staging area is and how to find it. I try to find them while winter scouting if at all possible. These areas will usually be pockmarked with what I call "cluster" rubs.

This isn't a rub line. It's not a long ridge with several rubs that lead from some point to another. This is an area where the rubbing seems random and highly concentrated. It's very common to mistake these spots for bedding areas, but usually you can differentiate a staging area from a bedding area by looking at how close it is to the nearest destination food source.

When I find what I believe is a staging area, which often involves islands of high ground in swampy terrain or ridges overlooking agricultural fields, I take a look around. If the rubs are in a spot that relates well to a food source and would give the deer a chance to either see a field or scent-check it without having to leave the cover, then you know you've probably found a staging area.

If the alders are torn up everywhere in a small area or there is a ridgetop that has been thrashed up, that means at least one buck was comfortable enough to spend some time there. It's obvious when you find it, and because staging areas are located in the cover, you can make an educated guess that the buck—or multiple bucks—was there during shooting hours. This is not the case with a field-edge rub, which easily could have been made at midnight. That's the whole point of finding staging areas. You want a spot to hunt where the bucks will move during shooting hours, during a time of the season when it can feel like they are all nocturnal.

If you haven't identified a few of staging areas while winter scouting, don't worry. You can find them during the season. You just need to walk quietly and keep your eyes peeled for a concentration of buck sign in the woods.

The area that I snort-wheezed in that Wisconsin public land buck a few years ago was a classic staging area. It was a patch of overgrown clear cut located between a distant agricultural field and a series of ridges where the deer like to bed. I didn't find it through winter or summer scouting, however. I found it through observation.

There are some situations where you simply won't find tons of buck rubs in a single area, but the deer are still using it heavily. The best way to know this is to watch. Every year I hang multiple stands with the idea that I'm mostly sitting to observe. This is hard to do, but it pays off enough to justify sitting where the odds of flinging an arrow are low.

With that Wisconsin buck, I hung and took down several stands throughout the property but always saw deer using one specific ridge. I ended up having to backtrack that ridge and then move into a creek bottom to watch it. The first buck I saw was a chocolate-racked eight-pointer that was obviously mature. He crossed the creek and made a few small rubs before sauntering down the ridge and out of sight.

I also saw several does, and every deer that came through within sight crossed the creek at the same spot. It took a couple of morning and evening sits to get it right, but eventually I moved my stand to an oak tree on the ridge closest to the crossing. The first morning I sat there, I tagged out an hour into the sit on a good buck.

After that hunt, I went back and walked the ridge. Several times, in fact. What I saw fully confirmed my belief that those public deer felt safe in that spot and they used it as an area where they could browse away while waiting to travel to, or as they traveled from, the only field within miles. That particular spot is probably at least 500 yards from the destination food source, but that's because it's a big-woods scenario. In ag-heavy areas, I find staging areas much closer, sometimes within 50 yards or so of the buffet.

The key to finding and hunting staging areas is to understand why the deer use them. This boils down to how advantageous the terrain is. As I've stated, they'll be able to see or smell what's going on in the destination food source from a staging area without having to poke their noses in the open.

Another thing to consider with staging areas is that we often feel that deer travel in a linear way. That is, we imagine they get up from their beds and walk straight to the food source, or in the mornings they reverse their travels in more or less a straight line.

This is an easy way to think about whitetail movement, but it doesn't do you much good. They don't just light out straight across the landscape most of the time. Instead they tend to go where they can fill their bellies and not be eaten. This might mean they bed in one area, walk parallel or away from the destination food source, and then eventually work their way toward the groceries at dark. Somewhere in there they'll kill some time, and that's where you need to be in October.

And that's something you'll find through spring scouting and in-season observation. So don't give up on early to mid-October just yet. Consider that most bowhunters will, and that means that while the world of the whitetail is changing daily, most hunters don't care. They aren't going to be out there, which will give you the opportunity to spend some time on common ground figuring out just what patch of cover the bucks like to spend their time in. That is the place where you'll be able to kill one when conventional wisdom says it's not going to happen.

10

KEEP SMILING, EVEN IF YOU WANT TO CRY

I hit my first breaking point with whitetails when I was fourteen. I'd hunted them hard, nearly every day after school and multiple times each weekend for three full seasons, and had come up with a big goose egg. It sucked. A lot. What made matters worse was that my dad had buddied up with a group of guys who didn't shoot does.

They were bowhunters from the old guard who lived by the belief that you weren't a man unless you killed bucks, and bucks only. Never mind the fact that most of the bucks they shot were absolute dinks, and the leader of the group, a one-eyed lunatic who is still the only person I know who has full on crapped his pants in a treestand, would shoot the very first yearling buck that came by no matter what. Maybe I'm being a bit unfair to the situation overall, because I did have a lot of fun being around those guys and that probably counts for something, but it was a toxic situation for a beginning bowhunter who didn't know what he was doing.

I wanted to shoot does, fawns, or whatever, but it was frowned upon. Eventually, the greed for a filled tag caused me to shoot at antlerless deer even when I knew I'd be ridiculed. Unfortunately, I couldn't hit them. There is probably some unfortunate soul out there who has suffered from buck fever worse than yours truly, but maybe not. I've had it bad.

So bad, in fact, that I was ready to give the whole thing up by the time I had three seasons under my belt. I wanted to shotgun hunt just to kill one, but in the end, I couldn't bring myself to do it. I threw a pity party for a few weeks but realized that I'd rather hunt than not, so I climbed back into a stand and kept bowhunting.

Eventually, I started hitting deer, some of them well, and my attitude smoothed out. Things were chugging right along until I turned 28, and then the pressure of being in the hunting industry got to me. That old, ugly habit of not being able to hit a deer came back with a vengeance. It was brutal.

Knowing that I'd have a short career as a bowhunting writer if I couldn't bowhunt worth a damn, I reinvented my shooting style and approach to the whole thing. It was a long process, but it worked. Both times, and I'm sure many others that I have repressed deep into the place where really bad memories go, caused me to hate the thing I love the most. And that's no good.

Attitude is a crazy thing. I'm not going to go full on hippie here, but there's an awful lot to be said about staying positive. A good attitude goes a long way toward enjoying the ups and downs of bowhunting, as well as throughout life in general. We all know people who have a junk attitude, and it's not terribly hard to understand why they have a hard life. It's a self-fulfilling prophecy to go around believing everything is going to end up crappy.

This, as you can probably guess, is also a bad way to go about trying something as challenging as bowhunting whitetails on public land. If you believe you won't kill a deer, I've got bad news for you: you won't. The best you'll do, which isn't any good at all, is screw up encounters with deer in such a way that you'll make things a hell of a lot worse.

I've got a pair of hunting buddies who are opposites in a lot of ways, but one glaring difference is their attitudes toward hunting success. The buddy with far less hunting experience always has a positive attitude during our public land trips, while the other guy doesn't. The other guy would be out of the game if he had one screw-up on day one of a weeklong hunt. He'd carry that sour demeanor with him in camp and in the field, and it wouldn't do him any favors.

The positive buddy, who should have been far less successful, wasn't. He killed more deer than his more experienced campmate, and I'm here to tell you the only reason that it shook out that way was because of what was going on between his ears.

It got so bad that I wrote an article about it for *North American Whitetail* magazine, thinking neither of my friends would see it. It turns out that a young bowhunter at the local lumberyard read it and showed it to my poor-attitude buddy when he stopped in for some two-by-fours one day.

We then had a heart-to-heart about life in general, and bowhunting in particular. That year, he killed his first out-of-state whitetail and his first mule deer. It may have been a coincidence, but he'd hunted both quite a bit and hadn't arrowed either during many previous attempts. To do it both in one year was an accomplishment, which I firmly believe can at least be partially attributed to attitude.

He's since gone on to become a killer, and I'll be honest, I didn't think that it would happen with him. Having some success and having to face the fact that he was negative for no good reason flipped a switch in him, and he's simply become deadly in the woods. The transition was incredible.

Here's the thing about staying positive while bowhunting public land: *you have to*. You have to dig deep into where us bowhunters keep our spare reserves of optimism and believe there is a chance your luck will change with the next sit. Or in the next few minutes on stand. It most often doesn't, but just often enough it does, and that can go a long way for our mental health.

It's easy to slip into a whitetail-induced state of depression, particularly after a couple of weeks of hunting, but try to avoid it. Don't lose any sleep over another hunter walking into your setup half an hour before dark, or if you should happen to whiff on a great deer.

It happens. Move on.

I always tell myself, when I'm starting to wig out about not being able to kill what is basically a glorified rabbit with antlers, that the success rate in general is very low. In most states, bowhunters have a success rate of about 15 to 30 percent. That means even in the best states, seven out of every 10 of us will eat tag soup when the season closes.

Now, factor into those statistics that state-wide success includes all bowhunters, not just those of us on public ground. If you were to find out the actual success rate of archery hunters who only hunt public ground, you'd probably sell your bow and buy some golf clubs.

It's probably well below 10 percent. The good news is that we don't hunt solely to kill a deer, or at least most of us don't. If you want to keep it that way, don't start filming your hunts for a television show. Trust me.

Most of us take to the woods for multiple reasons, just like most of us shoot certain deer for multiple reasons. We like to boil things down to its simplest form, like being a trophy hunter versus being a meat hunter, but that doesn't do anyone any real justice. It's a cheap debate trick at best.

Most of us hunt because we love being in the woods and we love seeing all animals (not just deer). My house is filled with loud ladies, so I love the outdoors because it's peaceful. I also love antlers as trophies and venison in my freezer. Try to remember what gets you out there and recognize all of the reasons if you get into a place of whitetail depression.

And also remember to stop comparing your life to others. Some people got lucky and inherited 600 acres of sweet ground; others worked their butts off to get their land or opportunities. Some people are naturally skilled at hunting in a way that most of us couldn't fathom. The world is full of inequality, and that is not going to change no matter how much we as a society push for equality of outcome. The best way to stay happy as a hunter and a human is to recognize that reality, as well as to recognize how lucky we all are.

To have the free time and the means to engage in a hobby like bowhunting is a gift. If you have to hunt public land, or choose to, recognize that gift as well. We have millions of acres that are open to us where we can do what we love. It may not be as easy as hunting some tightly controlled southern Iowa whitetail sanctuary, but I can promise you this: if you go out and work hard all season to kill a 100-inch buck on public land, it will mean a lot to you.

If someone puts you on a deer that has been raised to be shot when he's mature, it won't mean that much. I've done enough television hunts and guided hunts for media obligations to believe that to be 100 percent true. I'm not saying that the easier deer is totally devalued and it's not an enjoyable experience, because it certainly can be.

It's just not as rewarding. There is something about working hard toward a goal and eventually achieving it that we are hardwired to love. This goes for completing a marathon, building a house, or arrowing a buck where anyone can hunt.

11

RUT HUNTING AND THE IDIOT FACTOR

There are two great lies that have been perpetuated on the bowhunting public. The first is that we can look at a buck and know its age. The only real way to know a wild buck's age is to send in a tooth and have it aged through the cementum annuli method, and even then the results will be spot-on about 85 percent of the time. That's pretty much it, though. Looking at tooth wear, a sagging belly, antler size—it's all just a guess. And it's not even an educated guess most of the time, although we like to think it is.

I don't know how often I hear about 3.5-year-old bucks that are 170 inches and chock-full of world-record potential. Usually this comes from the deer-growing segment of the hunting population. There are no 3.5-year-olds that big in the wild. Or at best, somewhere, there is maybe one. But probably not.

The same thing happens with 2.5-year-olds. Or what people believe are 2.5-year-olds. How often does someone claim a buck is 2.5 because it has a narrow face or a lithe body even though it's sporting a 125-inch rack? All the time.

In both cases, I always wonder why we don't run into more 300-inch bucks in the wild. After all, if all these 3.5-year-olds are 170 inches, what do they turn into when they are fully mature and 6.5 years old? For some reason, those bucks must put on 93 percent of their antler growth in their first three years and then just stall out, right?

I can remember a very well-known hunting celebrity showing me trail-camera images of a nontypical buck that was all of 200 inches. He said it was off limits because it was only 3.5 years old. As far as I know, he never killed a 400-inch buck on his farm, but it's safe to assume that deer would have grown to astronomical proportions. It didn't, of course, because he was wrong.

I've gone off on a tangent here, and for that I apologize.

The second myth that is perpetuated on the bowhunting public is that the rut is the answer to all our problems. For example, if you can't kill a deer consistently with a bow outside of November, you just have to wait until all the lust-crazed bucks can't help but cover every inch of the county in search of amenable girlfriends.

If this were the case, I firmly believe that bowhunting success rates would be much higher. Now, if you take a competent bowhunter and put him in a decent woods during the second week of November, watch out. There is probably going to be a blood trail worth following before he needs to return to work.

The rut *can* be awesome. I love it, and you should too. But here's the thing: every one of us loves the rut. In deer country, there is probably more PTO burned up in November than any other time of the year.

What that means for the public land bowhunter is that he will have company. Potentially lots of it. My buddies and I affectionately refer to this as the "idiot factor." Now, I don't want to sound like a total prick here, but the thing is, bowhunting public land during the rut is kind of like trying to launch a boat at noon on July 4th at a popular, single-lane ramp. That experience can turn a seasoned fisherman's hair gray in a single shot.

I really do get that the level of experience in our ranks varies a lot, and I don't begrudge anyone for not really knowing how to bowhunt. We were all at that stage at one point, but even with that level of leniency I still witness and hear about behavior that baffles me.

One example occurred a few years ago in Nebraska. To be honest, I wasn't even in Nebraska when my hunting partner, who I was to meet on November 5th, called me up and said there was another bowhunter on the property who was hunting off his dirt bike. Aside from that being illegal, he was cruising around at daylight and throughout the evening when most of the deer should have been active.

This probably doesn't come as much of a surprise, but the deer didn't respond well to the Dirt Bike Kid. It wasn't until I was driving down there that my buddy called to tell me he heard the local game warden having a conversation with the dirt biker and that the activity had stopped. By the time

I got there, it was quiet.

Too quiet. I set up in one of my best public land spots and saw a single doe fawn. The following morning, I saw her again. It was hot, really hot for the rut, but there should have been a few bucks cruising around. I decided to make a move to the creek bottom, which I usually don't hunt, just to see if I could catch a thirsty buck making the rounds.

I sweated my way into the thick stuff and set up on a tiny clearing marked by rubs and scrapes. Fifteen minutes later the most miserable-looking buck I've ever seen walked by, and I shot the six-by-four at about 10 yards.

After butchering him in camp the next morning, I spent the rest of my time scouting for my buddy. The property, as usual, was covered in deer sign. I don't know what it is about Nebraska deer, but they leave a lot of scrapes and rubs in their wakes. While having deer sign is nice, it doesn't do you much good if the deer that left it have been run out of the ground on which you can hunt. I've never seen such a deer desert in my life, and I've got years of experience on the property, which tells me it was most likely the actions of a single person that changed the whole property for at least four or five days.

We did eventually find a few bucks that were bedding on nearby private land and working their way to the public, but my buddy never connected. I really believe one hunter on a dirt bike ruined that hunt for him, nearly for me, and for anyone else who tried to bowhunt immediately following his attempts to motocross his way into a buck.

If you spend enough time bowhunting public land, you'll have stuff like this happen. Dealing with the general hunting public isn't much different than dealing with the general public a lot of times, which is unfortunate.

What's worse is that during the rut, most bowhunters break out their bag of tricks. That means the grunt tubes will be honking, the antlers will be slammed together with alarming frequency, and the woods will be saturated in the hottest doe urine money can buy.

One of the biggest bucks I've arrowed in my life, a private land 10-pointer from Iowa, ended up wearing my tag because the buddy with whom I'd gained permission to bowhunt the farm was a rattling fool. He's an Iowa resident, so he's used to hunting during the rut in a state where the rut carries on uninterrupted.

I could hear him clacking away 400 yards downstream from the creek on which we'd both set up on in the morning. I had only seen one tiny buck, a deer that happened to breed a doe in front of my buddy while standing in the middle of the creek, when, at 9 a.m., I caught sight of a big deer trotting my way.

When the 150-incher got to 20 yards I stopped him and sent an arrow straight through his shoulder. Normally an iffy proposition, the penetration was good enough to reach his offside leg and all of the important stuff in-between. I firmly believe that deer didn't want anything to do with the near-constant buck brawls that he could hear raging on across the creek.

While I don't want to discourage anyone from trying something that might spruce up their hunt, I have to say this: you still have to do the work. Even when you're hunting the best time of the season—the rut—you're still going to have to out walk and outhunt the competition. If you do the necessary work to get in the spots that deer like and other hunters don't, then you can bust out the calls and other products that promise to bring bucks in like they are hypnotized.

And it's not like pressure is always bad. It can work to your advantage, but you have to understand how to use it. I can remember sitting in a tree in North Dakota on Halloween weekend one time watching what can only be described as a "deer tornado." I've never seen anything like it outside of that one magical evening.

The deer were staging across the river when one of the bucks started chasing. Now, I should say that the previous evening I had missed two bucks —a 120-incher and a solid mid-150s buck on which I totally delaminated. So I was already in a fragile state, but the odds seemed good that the tornado would work its way across the river into my lap.

For a few minutes it just stayed there, spinning in a crazy circle that was punctuated by white tails held high. And then the first buck crossed. The spike got a pass as he walked by. Then a decent eight-pointer put his hooves into the river, and I thought he probably wasn't going to be granted the same clemency as his two-pointed buddy. As he neared, however, a third buck stepped into the water.

That buck was good enough to get me to let the second buck walk, and when he got within range I shot him square in the guts. He hunched up in the river as the rest of the deer crossed and the light slipped out of the Badlands. I took the long way around, knowing I needed to leave him for the night. It was a night that I thought of him a lot, thinking of how someone who has arrowed so many deer in his life could so badly screw up an easy shot.

At first light I was back, following a sparse blood trail. It didn't take long before I found fresh coyote tracks and completely lost the blood. I don't know where the song dogs pushed that buck, but I know I didn't find him, and it wasn't for a lack of trying. I gave him from dark to dark and never located so much as a piece of hide.

It was a brutal lesson and a terrible finish to one of the best rut hunts of my life. I'm confident that the only reason I had so much action was because I had hiked a long way over a washed-out two-track to reach a spot most other hunters won't go. They used to, back when the two-track was in good shape. I know this because I saw them, or evidence of them, in that area all the time. They came by four-wheel drive, ATV, and horseback. Now, it seems, they just don't come.

They do hunt downriver, a mile and a half away, and it seems that the local ungulates know all about that, so they move on down.

Of course, once in a while, you just get lucky and run into one of those lust-crazed, tall-tined morons of the deer herd who is so blinded by his desires that he just decides to forgo his wary ways and trot through the woods. This is the buck that you have to pin your hopes on, because you will encounter other hunters when the rut is on and you're hunting where anybody can hunt.

Remember that deer, or deer like him, when you're frustrated by full parking lots and the not-so-distant sounds of rattling antlers. If you have done your homework and put in the requisite amount of work for your setups, you can outhunt the competition even when they are in danger of spilling over into your best spots. You just have to either ride out the pressure and wait for a hot doe to change your prospects, or find a place that the competition just isn't interested in hunting and spend a lot of time there.

Eventually, if you do, you might be rewarded with a shot opportunity while the rest of the hunters wonder where all of the bucks have gone, or maybe if the rut hasn't really started yet.

12

PROTEIN RETRIEVAL WITHOUT THE HEART ATTACK

Hopefully, by the time the rut has come and gone you've filled your tags and are off doing something else with your time. If you have, congratulations. I'd also like to know how the drag went when you did arrow a buck, because that task on public land can be a horrible, no-good experience. Or it can be easy.

Or something in-between.

When you've navigated a blood trail to your prize, you come upon the most satisfying and worst part of any hunt: the drag. Private land hunters can often fire up the four-wheeler and drive to their kill. Good luck with that on public land.

Now, I know there are public parcels that allow ATVs, UTVs, and other vehicles, but in my experience a lot of those are out west where the whitetail isn't exactly king (or even an afterthought for most hunters).

In the Midwest, East, and South, you're probably going to have to get a deer out the old-fashioned way, which is where the control-what-you-can-control advice comes in from Chapter Seven. Being in shape helps a lot when you've got 175 pounds of dead deer to remove from the forest, but so does the right plan and the right equipment. If you have to drag a buck and aren't in tip-top shape, admit it and seek out some help if there is any help available. Take your time to do it right. A lot of people get in a rush on a deer drag, but that's a mistake.

Hurrying through a physically demanding job when you're not ready for it is a great way to get injured or, occasionally, worse. I'm sort of obsessed with the idea of how we view ourselves and the biases we attach to those views. I don't think there is any greater lie we tell ourselves—and truly believe—than how physically fit we are. Most of us imagine that what we can accomplish is something far greater than reality. This happens, I think, because we rarely have to prove it.

It's kind of like the dude sitting at the bar watching cage fighting on television and causally commenting that he could hold his own against those professional athletes. He may believe that, but he also knows he's not going to step into the octagon and throw down any time soon. Or the middle-aged, pot-bellied guy who sees a beautiful younger woman and firmly believes that if he made the right moves, she'd be putty in his hands. Right... The difference between those two examples and shooting a deer three-quarters of a mile deep on public land is that you might actually do the last one. And then you've got to get it out, so have a plan.

If you're solo, like I am on an awful lot of my hunts, you'll need to plan your drags accordingly, because if you're doing it right on common ground, you'll be a long way from your truck. I had this experience a few years ago in Nebraska and was faced with either dragging my buck up a bluff and then across an easy ridgetop for almost a mile, or for a much shorter distance but through choking cedars along a creek. I opted for the bluff, which was the worst uphill drag I've ever had.

At one point I had to sit down on the hillside, pull the buck up a foot, and then scoot up a foot myself. It was the only way I could move him, and the only way I could keep my hands on him and ensure that he wouldn't roll all the way back down. A conservation officer stopped by camp when I was butchering the buck and asked me where I shot it. When I told him, he asked how I got it out. He didn't believe me at first, because he couldn't fathom anyone dragging a deer up that bluff with a helper, let alone solo.

The better bet than just digging in your heels and nearly killing yourself, at least in a lot of situations, is to use a game cart. Get a good one, and you'll be really happy. Buy a cheapie that doesn't have the right wheels and the proper balance, and you'll think game carts are pretty frickin' stupid.

I can remember my father building a game cart with the front tire of my BMX bike when I was a kid. I'd outgrown the bike, so he repurposed the front forks and wheel and built a wooden frame to attach it to. It was sort of like a flat wooden wheelbarrow that was too high off the ground and essentially balanced like a three-foot-tall unicycle. Loading a deer on it, even the little deer that were all we shot then, was a challenge that would leave you sweating, cursing, and oftentimes a little bloody.

If you did get your deer strapped to it, then you had to navigate the landscape with it. Imagine being forced to take 14 shots of tequila and then having to walk a tightrope. That would probably be easier than it was to get a deer out of the woods with the homemade cart my dad had conjured up.

I eventually bought a real cart, one with two wheels and an axle and the right design. It's one of my favorite purchases ever. If I have relatively open ground, or even open woods, I can pull a deer out with that cart easily. If I'm anywhere near a logging road or a two-track, it's even easier.

Even solo, with a good cart you can make short work of that mile in no time. If you don't currently have one but might be able to use one at some point while plying public land for your next buck, buy one. You won't regret it, and if you take decent care of it, your new cart will last a long time. I keep mine in the back of my truck or at camp at all times when I'm hunting in a place where I might be able to use it.

Unfortunately, sometimes you can't use a cart. Walk-In Areas oftentimes prohibit the use of any types of wheels, which means carts are a no-no. Your buck might just be discourteous enough to die in the middle of a washout or in a pond. I've had both happen, and neither was much fun. At this point, it's time to go western if you can.

Most states allow you to bone out a deer and pack it, elk-style. This is a process that isn't all that common amongst whitetail hunters. That's a shame, because it's awfully nice to be able to do when it's needed. I've only done this a few times, and it's a great way to get your meat out (and can easily be accomplished in two trips at most).

It does take a big pack and a good knife or two. I tend to keep a good-sized, 5,000-cubic-centimeter pack in my truck all season, along with an assortment of knives and sharpeners stashed under the seat. I also keep a box of one-gallon zip-seal bags in there as well. If I need to piece out a buck, I can do it after walking back to the truck and swapping out some gear.

If you know what you're doing, it's a matter of maybe an hour. And if you're a home butcher like I am, you were going to do that part anyway. If you don't butcher at home, don't worry. It's just an hour and nothing to gripe over.

Before digging in, you do need to know what you're doing. I've been on more than a few hunts with folks who didn't have a clue how to piece out their deer. That's always interesting to watch. There are plenty of tutorials on the internet where you can pretty quickly get the gist of how to separate a deer into manageable chunks. Watch them well before your hunt. If you usually bring your deer to a butcher to have him break it down to various meats, consider doing a couple yourself. It's an invaluable skill to have, and it really becomes something else if you need to do it deep in the bush or suffer the wrath of a hellacious drag.

Sharp knives are a must, and so is a workable surface area. I try to keep a small, six-foot-square tarp in my truck for this task. It weighs nothing and provides a nice little spot to place meat without worrying about contaminants. You can, in a pinch, use the hide of the deer, but that can be tough. Since it'll be attached to the carcass while you work on one side of the deer, it's always moving. In addition, the fat on the inside of the hide tends to grab a hold of all the dirt and sticks and grass it can, so it doesn't stay clean for long. Bring a tarp. You won't regret it.

You'll also need to think about a backpack that will actually work for the process. As I've mentioned, your choice should be good-sized. Most whitetail daypacks are a poor choice for hauling out deer quarters, but you don't need a full-on $600 frame pack for this task, either. A midlevel, midsized pack that is comfortable and adjustable is all you need. You'll probably have to make two trips for a decent-sized deer. It can be done in one, but I don't recommend it. That's a miserable experience.

We've all heard from our elk-hunting buddies about how they packed 125 pounds on their back at one time. But they probably didn't. They may not be outright lying, because they probably believed they were carrying that much, but most likely they were not. It probably wasn't even close.

A 75-pound pack is no joke. Absolutely no joke. If you don't believe that, grab your pack and throw 75 pounds of free weights in it. Then go climb a hill or a few flights of stairs. I packed a full buck's worth of meat, as well as his head, and my bow and camera gear one time out of a drainage in South Dakota. I don't know what it weighed, but it was a lot. Faced with that again, I'd pack him in two trips.

If you'll be hunting out of a camp, you've got another option: game bags. Game bags are popular in elk and moose country, but not so much where whitetails are king. I've used a variety of game bags over the years, but for deer I opt for a full-body game bag. Naturally, this doesn't go around the deer until I get it back to camp, but once there I can cover my deer in an antimicrobial game bag that is designed to wick away body heat.

This is a must when I'm hunting states with really early openers. It works wonders at keeping not only dust off the meat, but also flies. I've killed whitetails when the temperatures were in the 90s. As you can imagine, it doesn't take long for the flies to find a freshly killed deer then.

This is also a great time to lose meat if you're not careful, so in addition to having a plan on how to get your deer out if you're successful, you also need to have a way to get the meat cooled.

I shot a buck one time in the beginning of September in North Dakota that opened my eyes to the necessity of having a surefire way to cool off meat. Where I killed him, I knew I could get to the town of Medora in maybe 45 minutes, so I wasn't stressed out about being able to find some ice. The problem was that the resident elk season opened up the day after archery deer kicked off, and that meant that those successful elk hunters were also burning through serious ice.

I had to cover an embarrassing amount of miles to find anyone who had ice left, and it wasn't much fun. I didn't lose any meat because I started with enough ice to cool down the venison after the initial butcher process, but I definitely would have had trouble if I hadn't found someone to sell me fresh ice after a couple of days.

Another consideration to make is that with chronic wasting disease infecting deer throughout the country, most states won't let you import uncleaned skulls, spinal columns, etc. To stay on the right side of the law these days, if you're a traveling hunter, you almost have to know how to piece apart a deer.

This might also involve the knowledge of how to cape a buck. If that's not your thing and you don't want to prep your kill for a mount but do want to put the buck on the wall, you'd better have a taxidermist lined up before you send an arrow deer-ward.

The bottom line is this: you need to plan for game retrieval and venison care. Suffering a major chest grabber or losing your meat is best avoided at all costs, so you've got to have an extraction and a meat-care plan whether you'll be hunting with a few buddies or going at it solo.

13

LAST-GASP HUNTING IN THE LATE SEASON

If you think hunting public land in general is pretty tough, wait until you set your sights on a mature buck during the last few weeks of the season. If there is a greater bowhunting challenge that is realistic for average hunters to take on, I've never heard of it.

I know plenty of whitetail experts will talk a big game about how good the late season is, but those guys aren't setting foot on public land. They are hunting private ground with good food sources and limited, controlled pressure. They aren't hunting where you are, so their advice is total bunk.

In fact, so is mine. I've never killed a mature buck on public land with a bow during the late season. I've never even seen a legitimate 125-inch-plus buck, for that matter. I did have a spot in the Twin Cities where I could occasionally see a buck that was a great deer for public land, but even then we're talking maybe 100 to 115 inches. And if I'm being totally honest, I tried to put a few different people on those deer with muzzleloaders and couldn't make it happen.

A buck after a general firearms season is a different creature altogether. Gone are the risk-taking days of the rut or the early season when they might find themselves partially daft for one reason or another. December, or early January, is a perfect time for them to go truly nocturnal, and I believe an awful lot of them do.

The days are the shortest they'll be all year, which means bucks only need to hole up for nine or 10 hours. Then they are free to move and feed throughout a long night of wintry darkness.

There is always the chance, of course, that you could find one that will slip up. Or you could run into that mythical second rut, when the fawns should come into estrus. I've only seen evidence of that happening a few different times in 25 years of whitetail hunting, so it's not something I count on. It happens, and it's definitely cool when it does, but it's not something to rely on—especially on public dirt.

For this particular bowhunter, the late season brings with it something of an if-it's-brown-it's-down philosophy. I don't trophy hunt December on public land any more than I'd set my sights solely on dating swimsuit models if I were to find myself suddenly single. I know what the highest odds are of success, and I'm nothing if not a realist in at least some capacities of my life. Cast a wide net, I say.

To kill any deer on public land when it's cold and the snow is flying is a feat worthy of some chest thumping, so look at it that way. If you've got a doe tag left, hunt does. Or fawns. If you've got a buck tag, hunt bucks. Any bucks. You may feel as if you've read this somewhere recently…

Now, if I absolutely had to say what my best public land strategy is for hunting a buzzer-beater deer, it would be to get back to a staging-area plan. By about Christmas time, the deer seem to shake off a few of the jitters from gun season, and they may be caught traveling through the woods at first and last light in relation to a destination food source.

Where I spend a lot of my hunting time, those transition areas are cattail sloughs and just generally thicker forests. They want security cover, and they won't sprint into a cut cornfield with an hour of daylight left like you see so often on outdoor television. Survival is everything to them during this time of year, and one way they survive is by clinging to the best cover they have available to them and moving as little as they need to.

Hunting the edges of that cover, or sometimes right in the middle of it, is the best I've got. I've arrowed some deer doing this and have occasionally had some pretty cool hunts regarding deer movement and activity, especially if I've got the wind just right and there is a front coming in or heading out. If that front brought with it six inches of fresh powder, it's usually even better.

This is the time when details matter so much. This all starts with the right clothing to keep the wind at bay and allow you to harness as much body heat as possible. The more comfortable you are, the less you'll move and fidget. You also need to be able to maneuver into shooting position quietly and hold your bow at anchor exactly the way you would in July while wearing shorts and a T-shirt.

I was once sitting on a treestand along a creek bottom in Nebraska when I noticed a buck working his way in. He was on top of me about the time I got into position to draw. With one last movement to twist my torso in preparation to draw, a grommet on my boot caught on one of the support cables of my stand. It pinged off, and that buck turned inside out. When the woods are quiet and the deer are jaded from so many recent attempts on their lives, those types of mistakes always go in their favor.

This is also the time of year where you should ramp up your target shooting routine. It's easy to slack off on the shooting during the season, which is never a good idea. And it's really not a good idea after three months of hunting when you're planning to sit in chilly temps wearing bulky clothes. I don't know how many times over the years I've had something change on my bow due to routine in-season abuse, but it's enough to make me slightly neurotic over the possibility that my point of impact may suddenly be somewhere it shouldn't.

If there's an upside to late-season bowhunting on public land, it's that you'll probably have the woods to yourself, and you might get to wear snow camo. I don't know if there is a better combination of seasonal conditions and camouflage choice than late-season hunting in full snow camouflage when there is fresh powder on the ground. If you're going to get an advantage over the deer, that's it. It's little consolation, I know, but it's something.

If you're going to set your sights on a last-minute deer on public land, say your prayers, pick up a lucky rabbit's foot or three, and get ready to be humbled. At the same time, know that there is a possibility that a front will roll in, the deer will move 15 minutes before dark, and you might end up on the easiest blood trail of the year.

That possibility is enough to make it worth it.

14

LEARN TO CRAWL BEFORE ATTEMPTING TO SPRINT

Throughout this book, you've probably noticed I've referenced mostly bucks for the hunting strategies and tactics. This is intentional, but it's not totally indicative of my bowhunting focus.

I love bucks, but I also love does. I love watching them, hunting them, arrowing them, and, of course, eating them. The hunting industry doesn't give lady deer much attention, aside from their ability to produce bucks. That's a mistake in my opinion for a couple of reasons.

The first is that hunting used to be a personal journey of working through individual experiences and challenges to get better over years and years of experience. This usually started with small game hunting, then maybe transitioned to upland or waterfowl, and then finally culminated in deer and other species of big game.

No one started out hunting 160-inch deer. Today, that's not the case. A lot of hunters, too many in my opinion, come right out of the gate looking down on any deer that doesn't warrant an immediate post on social media and a trip to the taxidermist. I'm a firm believer in the old adage about learning to crawl before you learn to walk. In this case—at least metaphorically speaking—if you don't learn to crawl in the deer woods, you most likely will give up long before learning to walk.

The second reason why I love does is because if you can consistently earn shooting opportunities on them, you'll be able to master the buck game easily enough. Does that spend their time on public land have big targets on them the same as the bucks, and they have the burden of raising the next generation of deer.

They don't take this job lightly.

And because of that, they tend to be hard to kill. I firmly believe this, and I think the reason we don't look at them the same way, aside from the obvious fact that most of them don't grow antlers, is because we lump does into one category. They are just antlerless deer and nothing else.

The thing is, if you're looking to be a successful hunter and you only target bucks, you're really narrowing your chances to do things right or learn from your mistakes. The best hunters I know may not be the guys with a Super Slam to their name, but they are stone-cold killers.

They've gotten this way through years of hunting and finding success in the deer woods. This means they've killed their fair share of bucks, of course, but an awful lot of them have a pile of does to their credit.

This is no small thing.

Just think about how few times a bowhunter actually gets to take a shot in his or her career. Relative to the hours and days afield, it's a very small percentage of outings that result in an arrow being shot.

An even smaller percentage of the time, that arrow goes where it is supposed to. This means that if you're focused solely on bucks, or a specific size of buck, you might shoot one time per season. Some years, you won't shoot at all. It can certainly be done, but getting good at something you rarely do is tough indeed.

Now, I'm not advocating shooting every deer that walks by just to become a better bowhunter. What I'm saying is that every time you go into kill mode on an approaching deer, the whole situation morphs into something else.

It's no longer time to sit there, without moving, and watch as deer pass by your stand. Instead, it's time to clip on, possibly stand up to jockey into shooting position, and contemplate the ideal moment to draw. This is the time when plenty of sure-thing encounters change into events where the outcome is far from a certainty.

I really think that learning exactly when to draw is on par with knowing precisely where to aim as an animal walks through and the point of impact changes with each subtle movement it makes. It's that important.

The more times you do this and get it right, or get busted, the better you'll be moving forward. Bowhunting is an exercise that frequently results in failure. It just is. But the more comfortable you become in the situations where you have to do everything right, the less you'll experience failure.

The way to get to that point is to screw up a lot (while occasionally getting it all right). This goes for the moments leading up to the shot. This is often a little more difficult with a doe than a buck, because the ladies tend to travel in little packs, meaning more eyes, ears, and noses to beat.

If you can consistently find spots through which mature does travel on public land and can put yourself in a position to remain undetected throughout a shot sequence, then you are on one hell of a path to success with all deer (and many other game species as well).

What happens after the shot matters too, of course. Your job doesn't end with coming to anchor and triggering your release. You've got to be able to blood trail deer, and you'll get better at that the more you do it.

I don't know how many times I've had to blood trail with people who simply blundered ahead on the trail looking for a corpse, but it has happened a lot. It's a great way to get kicked off a blood trail by yours truly and not get invited back to camp.

I hate that behavior so much.

The vitriol I feel for lazy or haphazard blood trailing comes from experience. I've been on a lot of blood trails and have seen all kinds of crazy things happen. Generally speaking, the more you rush it, the higher the odds you'll lose the deer. Blood trailing should be a quiet, patient process that involves plenty of thinking, because it usually consists of equal parts logic and instinct.

The logic involves taking the actual spoor you're dealing with and using it to determine how to proceed. As you proceed, logic factors into rationally contemplating the likeliest routes through the cover that your deer could have traveled, where the nearest water is, which routes will take you uphill or down, etc.

Instinct, on the other hand, will guide you to make the best decisions possible, and that comes from experience. There have been quite a few times in my life where I've been stumped on a blood trail and have just had a thought pop into my head like, "Maybe he didn't go down this trail at all, but instead veered off a ways back to dive into that honeysuckle patch and bed down."

It doesn't happen every time, of course, but occasionally one of those sent-from-the-heavens ideas will pay off, and you'll make a decision that leads right to a deer that has given you the slip a few times already.

What does all this have to do with hunting does? A lot.

The more times you take a shot and have to follow up on it, the better you'll get. It's much easier to get better at hunting overall—and shooting deer specifically—if you're open to the idea of trying to put a doe or two in the freezer.

Plus, it's more fun to have options.

One of the reasons I love driving 14 or 15 hours to Oklahoma to hunt whitetails on public land is because the state is full of deer. It is becoming more well-known for churning out good bucks than in the past and is often referred to as a sleeper state, but the draw for me is being able to shoot a whole bunch of deer on my nonresident license.

I love getting into a stand in the Sooner State knowing that any deer that walks by is a potential shooter, and that if I do thump a doe, it's not going to affect my chances to hunt the following day because I've still got the option to shoot more. That's just a more enjoyable hunting situation to get into than some of the bag limits in other states, particularly northern states with lower deer populations and fewer tags.

A few years ago a couple of buddies and I went down to Oklahoma to hunt the season opener at the beginning of October. Aside from the six days of near-constant rain soaking us and our tents, the oversized spiders, and the fact that I almost castrated myself on a barbed-wire fence that broke when I was crossing it, the trip was a blast.

This was due in no small part to the fact that we averaged a deer kill a day for three bowhunters. On public land that we'd never been to before, that's pretty impressive. Granted, we weren't killing 170-inchers. But we were filling up our coolers with plenty of fresh venison, and we did get the opportunity to stoke up our little charcoal grill each night to cook the freshest protein a modern American is likely to sink his teeth into. At least for this particular bowhunter, that's not nothing.

I ended up arrowing two mature does on that trip. One was out of a treestand on opening night. She made a bad decision to pose up at maybe 10 yards when deciding where to spook after some other hunters drove by and stopped to look at the bucks I was watching.

The other doe I killed was in a spot that just looked too good to not at least spend a morning or two in. But if I'm being honest, part of the reason I hunted the area was because it was frequented by a big flock of turkeys. I saw them while driving to camp one day for lunch, and when I went in to investigate, not only did I realize that the turkeys were thick in there, but that there seemed to be a fair amount of deer using it as well.

That's a twofer in my book.

In addition to having plenty of deer tags and our eyes peeled for a feral pig, we also had the opportunity to shoot a turkey if it happened to wander by (a threefer?). So one morning I slipped into a really cool spot near a state-planted food plot to see if I could call in some birds off the roost while also keeping an eye out for a deer.

As I huddled into a natural blind and it started to get light, I spotted a bonus shed antler on the ground next to me, which doesn't happen very often. At the same time, the turkeys were becoming more and more vocal, but they gave off a noncommittal vibe when I asked them to come my way. I was enjoying our conversation just the same when I heard a stick snap behind me. The doe didn't quite know what to make of the camouflage lump sitting in the middle of a deadfall, but she definitely didn't trust it.

Unfortunately for her, she got distracted just long enough for me to draw and settle my pin. One of my hunting partners and I found her after a short blood trail. It's one of my favorite hunting memories, simply because of how beautiful a morning it was and how it all played out.

And it was all made possible by a lowly old doe.

As you head out for another season on public land, don't forget the does if you can get an antlerless tag or three, because hunting them isn't as easy as we like to make it sound. And if you do figure out how to put the matriarch of the herd in the back of your truck with any level of consistency, the bucks will be no problem at all.

15

THE AIR GUITARISTS OF THE HUNTING WORLD

The outdoor industry, and the bowhunting industry in particular, is full of people who are the equivalent of someone who is really good at playing air guitar. Stick with me here. To be a truly good guitar player, you have to love it, you have to devote countless hours to learning how to play, and you have to do it yourself. No one can play guitar for you.

The people in the hunting industry I'm referring to are like the weirdos who get on stage and rock out to a song while flailing their arms around and pretending to play guitar. When they kill a big buck (the hunters, not the air guitarists), they most likely had someone do all the work for them. This starts with finding a place to hunt, scouting, hanging stands, etc. Then this air-guitar joker shows up, is told where to sit, goes in, and arrows a buck. They are triggermen (and, increasingly, women), and they are a far cry from the type of hunter who grinds it out on public land for an entire season.

These people, and I know quite a few of them, don't have any interest in 95 percent of what hunting actually is. They want to fill their trophy room quickly and with as little investment of time as possible. If you're part of the hunting industry, this is easier to do than you would imagine. Even a low-level writer like yours truly receives multiple invitations each season to go on free guided hunts. I've often thought about doing an experiment where I would accept each invite and then tally up how many animals I killed at the end of the season.

Fortunately, I just can't bring myself to do it.

As you can also guess, a lot of industry hunters jump at those chances and structure their entire careers around them. These people are a terrible example of what the average person should aspire to. If you want to be a good hunter, they aren't the ones to follow, because they aren't really even hunting. Someone else is doing the majority of the hunting for them, and they are just showing up to take the glory. Sound gross? It is.

That's how it works. The hunting industry offers one of the few jobs where you can be nearly talentless and still be considered a professional. You can't even do that in fishing, because eventually you have to compete against other anglers who do have skill, and you'll be found out. In hunting, you can skate along for years killing big animals you didn't work for, and somehow these triggermen get a pass. It's pretty crazy stuff.

I'll get off my soapbox now and finish this by saying you should be proud of what you do. If you work hard at it, you'll find success on public land. It's that simple. It may not be the 200-inch success of the one-percenters on TV, but that's okay. That's not reality any more than their hunting is, so don't aspire to it.

Aspire to enjoy your time afield, and to learn from the woods the many lessons it can teach. Aspire to take a few kids into nature and show them the same lessons. Hunt for happiness and to satisfy that gene-deep craving we all have for watching the sunrise in a forest.

Hunt for yourself and have fun.

Good luck.

www.ingramcontent.com/pod-product-compliance
Lightning Source LLC
Chambersburg PA
CBHW020456160726
47991CB00007B/2688